IF I CAN,
YOU CAN

TRANSFORMATION MADE EASY

DAVID ZELMAN, PHD

If I Can, You Can: Transformation Made Easy

Published by Wheatmark®
1760 East River Road, Suite 145
Tucson, Arizona 85718 USA
www.wheatmark.com

ISBN: 978-1-62787-326-0 (paperback)
ISBN: 978-1-62787-327-7 (hardcover)
ISBN: 978-1-62787-328-4 (ebook)
LCCN: 2015959035

rev201601

*This book is dedicated in part
to my mother and father, Shirley and Al,
the best parents in the world.
It is also dedicated to Wyatt.
You are my hope and commitment for the future.*

"If I create from the heart, nearly everything works."
—Marc Chagall

TABLE OF CONTENTS

WE CAN

FOREWORD

As a coach, consultant, keynote speaker, teacher, and workshop leader, I am constantly in search of a deeper access to my own creative power and ability to generate space for others to discover their power.

David Zelman's counsel and his Transitions Process ignite a flame of passion, purpose, and full self-expression for anyone willing to honestly look at themselves and engage in realizing their full potential as a human being. David's mastery of context, psychological theory, communication, and transformation is brilliantly presented in this book. *If I Can, You Can* expands the reader's understanding of how to live in a way that constantly generates growth, development, and future of one's own choosing.

At the Soul of Money Institute in San Francisco, we work with people of great wealth, as well as people who are struggling to make ends meet, and everyone in between. We have fully embraced the Transitions Process. Its simple yet powerful message—"the actions we take, and therefore the results we produce, are 100 percent correlated to our internal conversations"—provides us with a freedom to focus on what's important and avoid getting sidetracked by all the distractions that constantly interrupt our mission. Knowing that we are the authors of our lives, our actions, and our commitments has nourished, honored, and fertilized our work. Our ability to transform our own consciousness, to transform the consciousness of others, to leave our old identity behind, and to move into a place of true power is remarkable.

If I Can, You Can is not about self-improvement. It's not just another theory that might work for some. David has been transforming lives for more than thirty years, and this book is filled with real-life examples of how the process works.

The Pachamama Alliance is an organization, a movement, and an initiative that I love with all of my heart. It has been deeply impacted by David's partnership and participation. Pachamama means "mother earth." It is an alliance between indigenous peoples of the Amazon and the Andes, and conscious, committed people of the modern world for the sustainability of life. From rain forests in South America to corporate board rooms, there is an immediate need for all of us to raise our consciousness, to expand our capabilities and capacities, and to embrace each other and the planet itself.

In the first chapter of this book, David tells the remarkable story of his own journey. I want to let the reader know that he has continued to express his life as a creative masterpiece. His extraordinary marriage to his beloved wife Karen of 35 years is a relationship that is conscious and loving, and has the space to work out anything and everything. It is filled with joy, respect, and reverence for one another, and for the marriage itself. His three children, Michael, Lauren, and Brian, are all successful in their own right— emotionally, spiritually, psychologically, and financially. Their lives are their own creations, not based on circumstances, but rather on their creative power and capacity to generate a life they love.

David's circle of friends, which I am part of, is a remarkable testament to his love for people, his capacity to serve and support others, and his commitment to be the kind of man that not only generates his own life, but also generates the space for others to create their own lives.

The Transitions Institute and Dr. David Zelman are treasures in this world. This book and the words you will read will not only touch your heart, but will alter the very course of your life. If you take this seriously, and realize that the capacity to create the future sits in your hands right now, the words in this book will be magic for you. I am honored to invite you to engage as deeply as possible in *If I Can, You Can*. Because of David's life history, his deep experience, and his great wisdom, *we all can*.

Lynne Twist
Founder, Soul of Money Institute
San Francisco, CA
November 2015

ACKNOWLEDGMENTS

First, I want to thank Keith Hollihan and Howard Means for helping me transform my personal experience into words on a page. You are both brilliant and extremely gifted.

Thank you to Suzan Oran and Dr. Scott Conard for introducing me to Grael Norton and Wheatmark Publishing. Grael, you and your colleagues at Wheatmark (especially Lori and Mindy) have been immensely helpful and supportive.

To the Maharishi Mahesh Yogi and Werner Erhard, I am forever grateful. Werner, in particular, transformed my relentless search for meaning and happiness into a life of abundance, contribution, freedom, and joy. Thank you to Mark Zucker for all the times you were there as a friend when a friend was needed.

Over the past two decades, I have been blessed with a large group of friends and colleagues who never stopped encouraging me to write this book: Sol Gordon, Peter and Candice Olson, Dr. Choe, Kathi Becker, Al Zdenek, Jack Daly, and all my brothers and sisters from The Gathering of Titans (especially Rick Sapio). To those I owe so much in so many ways—Larry, Lori, Carl, Randy, Terry, Steve, Robin, Denise, Bill, Lynne, Ed, June, Ilan, Brandy,

Mike, Eric, Jess, Ken, Jill, David, Harianne, Ellen and Lew—thank you, thank you.

A special thanks to John, Elizabeth, Jan, and Skye for becoming my extended family and always feeding me power. John, you in particular make so much possible with your wisdom, generosity, and love.

To my assistant Marsha, you and only you know how much you contributed to this book. Thank you. To Tiff, what can I say? You are the best human being this world has to offer.

To my family—Al and Shirley, Bill and Marilyn, and Michael and Joanne, I'm so grateful knowing you always have my back.

To my amazing children—Michael, Brian, Lauren, and Bret, I love our love for each other.

Finally, to my beautiful wife Karen, yes it's true—I married up. I am blessed by our profound partnership, and I look forward to being with you every minute of every day.

IF I CAN

TRANSFORMATION MADE EASY

THE STORY BEGINS

My first recollection in life is that of my mother standing by my crib and wailing. I knew something was wrong, but I couldn't have possibly understood that she was crying uncontrollably over my nine-month-old sister, who had died shortly before my birth. My mother was crying over who I wasn't, not who I was. I strongly believe that some of my early psychological programming was formed on these occasions. The sense that something was wrong and that I was incapable of fixing it stayed with me for decades.

I don't think it takes much to have an infant or young child start on a course of self-doubt, insecurity, and need. We all have our childhood traumas. I guess some of us deal with them better than others do, but I'm sure that none of us emerges from childhood without psychological wounds and scars—most of which are buried or forgotten, but not completely gone. These negative experiences leave many of us cautious and wary. Still others seem to bounce back and apparently go on unscathed.

Regardless, my childhood can hardly be recalled as fun or joyful. I was preoccupied with death. My best friend at age five died from an infection or disease. My grandfather died fifteen minutes after a Sunday family dinner. (More wailing.) Life was scary.

I grew up in a home where my two brothers and I were clearly loved by our parents, but this added another dimension to the problem. I was hyperactive. (Today, we would call me ADHD and dyslexic.) I couldn't read a damn thing until fourth grade. I certainly never read at my grade level and struggled through school.

Unfortunately, sports didn't make me feel better about myself either. I sucked at baseball and basketball, which were the two most popular sports where I grew up. So I always felt that I was a disappointment and an embarrassment to my parents. This particularly stung because I idolized my father and never wanted to disappoint him.

The only thing I had going for me was that, for some reason, girls seemed to like me. While I can't recall what we discussed, I do remember I spent a lot of time on my home's front stoop talking to the girls in the neighborhood. And there were lots of them! So through no intention that I can discern, I learned a great deal about communication at an early age. The thing I learned best was to listen. I was fascinated at how these girls could talk about almost anything, particularly things I had no opinion or knowledge about. I also learned to dance. I probably was not a great dancer, but I had lots of dance partners at all the parties and socials. I grew up loving girls, not myself. I didn't have to compete with them, just play.

When I followed my best friend to the University of Cincinnati in 1965, my freshman year was predictable. I majored in drinking and partying, and minored in studying and going to class. Fortunately, my grades were just high enough for me to stay in school. Unfortunately, my friend didn't make the grade and returned to New York to attend college. Once there, he must have seen the light, because he graduated, went on to law school, and before going into private practice, was the assistant DA for a major East Coast city.

MY SOPHOMORE YEAR

Sophomore year started with a bang—lots of them, actually. In September 1966, the Vietnam War was a major influence on many US campuses. During the first weeks of the fall semester, I was introduced to pot at a party. It seems funny now. I wasn't out to be different or break the law. I was just trying to fit in. Someone handed me a joint and said, "Try this," and I did. For the next couple of years, I couldn't think of anything I'd rather do than get high.

In an instant, I saw myself, my friends, and my life differently. I went from being an insecure person who had no purpose and no future, with nothing to be proud of, to someone who, for no reason I can explain, just let all that crap go. I felt at home with myself and in love with my friends. Shortly after that, I found a purpose: protest against the injustice of the Vietnam War. I even wrote poetry and essays against the war. I still couldn't read at grade level, but I started writing to the campus paper and got a few of my writings published.

Without going into detail, I can say the next two years were about rebellion and defiance—against my parents and any form of authority. We took to the streets in Cincinnati; in Washington, DC; at Kent State; in San Francisco; and in Chicago ("Days of Rage"). If there was going to be an organized protest, I wanted to be there. And I wasn't alone. I was just one in the crowd. I wasn't a leader—actually, far from it—but I did belong. I was a part of a great movement that was exciting and, in our eyes, just.

I was also riding the wave of a reborn musical generation—the Stones, the Doors, the Beatles, Jimi Hendrix, Chicago, and Bob Dylan, just to mention a few. This was my life. I woke up into a daily drama that was going to unfold in drugs, music, antiwar demonstrations, and, again, absolute minimal schoolwork.

This lifestyle was untenable, however, and in 1968, I dropped out of school for the second time. I'd like to say I had important things to do, but in reality, if I hadn't dropped out of school, I would have failed and been thrown out.

WHERE TO GO? WHAT TO DO?

Having already burned my bridges at home in New York, I had few options. I had a cousin named Stephen who lived in Sausalito and had a good setup. That's where I headed, hoping he would help me in some way. He was a part of North Beach Leather on Telegraph Hill in San Francisco. All the great musicians came there for their leather pants, boots, jackets, sandals, and so forth.

Just hanging out in San Francisco was a trip. I had hoped to get a job there, but when that didn't work out, I went from party to party, new friend to new friend, not doing much of anything. It got really bad, and I was getting desperate. I got away from the David I grew up as in New York and away from the dissident in Cincinnati, but I didn't get away from my own psychodramas.

Without a clear future or a purpose to create something with my life, I started to get very concerned. These were my darkest days—bad thoughts, really bad thoughts. Not that I would intentionally hurt myself, but I was living an empty, meaningless existence.

Then a bit of a miracle occurred. Danny, a friend of mine, came out to San Francisco to visit. He was reading a book by Harry Stack Sullivan, a Neo-Freudian. By chance, I opened it and started reading. To my amazement, everything he wrote made sense. I felt as if I knew everything he was writing about. When I asked Danny where he got the book, he said it was a textbook from a psychology course he was taking. I was flabbergasted!

I asked, "You get tested on this?"

He said yes, and in that moment, I saw a possible future: go back to school and study psychology.

That is one of the most powerful sentences I have ever said to myself: "Go back to school and study psychology."

BACK TO SCHOOL

In the fall of 1969, the year I was originally going to graduate college, I started over, giving it everything I had. I had to work harder than anyone I knew. I had to spend countless hours in the library, but through sheer work and determination, I made the dean's list and actually got a 4.0.

My next stop was the University of Wisconsin. That was another school with a very strong antiwar culture, but by this time, I had completely stopped doing drugs of any kind. I began meditating (transcendental meditation), and you can't meditate effectively and get high.

You might say I have an all-in mentality. I got deeply into TM for the next eight years and still continue to mediate almost daily. I went to see the Maharishi, the founder of transcendental meditation. I took advanced classes and went on retreats. I went to monasteries and meditated for days. All the while, I was studying psychology and earning a PhD in behavioral disabilities.

DAVID ZELMAN, PHD

Life had definitely improved. I felt so much better about myself and my future. I was on a roll, achieving my goals, receiving my PhD, publishing my doctoral dissertation, and getting royalties. I was even on the speaker circuit. I had a great job as the staff development and training director for New Concepts Foundation, running more than fifty residential facilities for the handicapped throughout the state of Wisconsin. And I married a great woman, Jane.

Those were all on my to-do list, things I had to accomplish to be successful. I was doing such a great job meeting my goals and setting new ones that I didn't have a clue I was actually unfulfilled and simply feeding my ego. At least, not until the fall of 1976.

One of my friends had an A-frame home on the Wisconsin River. Someone needed to go on a beer run, and since I had a brand-new Saab EMS, I volunteered to go. Jeff came along to enjoy the ride in my new car. I thought this a great time to test a feature called antiskid geodynamic steering. Supposedly, if the car went into a skid and you released the steering wheel, the car would automatically correct for the skid and go straight. So I intentionally threw the car into a skid at sixty miles per hour. Unfortunately, the car rolled three times, throwing both Jeff and me into a cornfield.

The next thing I "remember" (not exactly, but I'll come to it shortly), I was in an ambulance, regaining consciousness and on the way to the hospital. Fortunately, we both survived.

I sustained the worst of the injuries: broken vertebrae, three broken ribs, and a concussion. The next ten days were spent in intensive care. I was happy to be alive but feeling beyond stupid, in a lot of pain, and, perhaps most importantly, feeling totally alone. Jane and my parents were there to support me, but somehow I felt distant, unconnected, and miserable.

Before the accident, I was in good physical shape, which helped me recover from my injuries over the next several months. But psychologically, I couldn't rally. Perhaps this is because of what occurred when I was ejected from the Saab into the cornfield. That experience is something I will never forget. Some describe it as a white-light experience, and that's how it occurred for me.

It was a comforting white light and a voice. (It sounded like a man's voice, but that's not important.) I was asked a very simple question: *Do you want to go back? If you do, it will be very painful.*

If that was dying, then dying is easy. No pain, no struggle—just a simple choice and surrender.

As you can guess because I'm writing this book, I chose to return. And I was instantly greeted by extreme pain and fear. I couldn't breathe (remember the three broken ribs). I couldn't move (remember the broken spine). And nothing made sense (remember the concussion).

For a long time, I interpreted "if you go back, it will be very painful" as referring to my physical condition, to experiencing physical pain. Little did I know that the real pain would come in the form of a rebirth, a transformation that would require giving up everything: my identity as a PhD, my marriage, my plodding through life, "making it." I would have to come to terms with the realization that all the symbols of success I had achieved, and still sought to achieve, would never bring a sense of fulfillment and accomplishment.

TRANSFORMATION

When the student is ready, the teacher will appear.

In October of 1976, Marshall Serwitz passed through Madison. We had been friends many years earlier back in New York. I respected Marshall. He seemed to be one of the few people I knew who had both oars in the water.

Now, here was Marshall telling me I had to do the EST training, a seminar that could help me gain control of my life. He said it would be great for me but couldn't say exactly how or why. The program cost $325 at that time, and I was sure it wasn't worth the money. I told him I was doing great and didn't need it. He was relentless, insisting that it would be worth my time and money. I said I didn't think I could afford it, so he offered to pay for Jane and me to attend. If it was that important to him that I do this EST training, well, what the hell?

In January 1977, Jane and I drove down to Chicago from Madison to take the course. All the way, my mind was screaming at me, telling me what a stupid idea this was. How could I let Marshall manipulate me this way? After going through grad school and getting a PhD, I was certain there was nothing I was going to hear that would be of any value.

To make matters worse, when I arrived at the hotel ballroom for the program, they wouldn't let me in the training room. "Why not?" I asked.

"Because you haven't completed your paperwork successfully."

I thought, "Shit! I know I'm going to hate this! I haven't even gotten in the room, and already I'm failing."

Before I was allowed into the room, one of the assistants coached me on declaring what my purpose for attending would be. In other words, what did I want to get out of the training? Halfheartedly, I wrote down what I thought they wanted to hear, plus a personalized kicker. I wrote that I wanted to feel better about myself, experience more intimacy in my marriage, and (the kicker) I wanted a better relationship with my German shepherd.

Finally, they let me in the door. I still wonder whether wanting a better relationship with my German shepherd is what got me in the room. Did I mention I was still in a back brace from my car accident? Because of this, I was allowed to sit in the back row and get up from time to time to stretch. There were three hundred people seated in the room, and for a while, I couldn't see Jane. Then I picked her out toward the front. I felt a little better. At least I wasn't alone.

A few minutes later, someone walked to the front of the room and addressed the group, asking questions and giving us some ground rules. Surprisingly and unexplainably, I actually liked what was happening—and what I liked was who the person was being. Totally confident. Totally clear. Totally present. I was intrigued.

Someone in the group raised their hand (that was a ground rule if you wanted to speak or ask a question) and challenged one of the ground rules about not being allowed to take notes. What happened next was the beginning of a long, hard, and extraordinary journey. From the back, another voice boomed into the room. It seemed like the guy in front was just the opening act. Now the real leader, or trainer (to use the group's terminology), stepped into the middle of the room. He said, "Our relationship with the ground rules of life suck. We don't have a clue. Our lives don't work, and we are lying to ourselves and everyone else."

Within fifteen minutes, I was 150 percent engaged. I felt like I had finally, accidentally, died and gone to heaven. This was an extraordinary paradox. I was thrilled with what was unfolding in the training room. That trainer, in front of three hundred people, embodied everything I wanted to be. His confidence, certainty, power, and presence were breathtaking. I wanted desperately to have what he had—to be like him—and in that moment I realized with astonishing clarity that I was not like him.

I was an actor, a fake, going through life pretending to be happy, strong, and successful. This was indeed a terrifying realization. I wanted to argue against it, but I knew it would be of no use. The genie was out of the bottle. There would be no going back.

Flooded with emotion, I didn't know whether to be happy or sad, inspired or fearful. Actually, it didn't matter what I wanted to experience. I quickly realized I didn't have a choice. I was on the ride of my life, and the best I could do was hold on and try to absorb as much as possible.

ENLIGHTENMENT

Enlightenment came with a price.

It seemed as though all three hundred of us in the training room were suffering from the same illusion, living unfulfilled lives, going through the daily motions of gathering evidence that things were okay, and kidding ourselves that things would be okay. We had all been operating in a condition of mass hypnosis, which we finally broke through, just as Neo did in the movie *The Matrix*.

Once freed from the effort and struggle to prop up a life that was never going to produce real joy and happiness, I discovered I didn't have to prove anything to anybody. I was free from judging others and myself and from trying to get somewhere or something.

And in that freedom, something extraordinary happened. A lifetime of experiences—in fact, my whole life—made sense. At first, it was so simple that I questioned whether it was real or if I was just fooling myself. Well, almost forty years later, I feel certain that I discovered my path, my life's purpose: *providing well-being for human beings.*

Looking back, I can see this theme, this thread, running throughout my life.

From early childhood, it was manifested when I was talking to the neighborhood girls on my stoop, but even before that, I can look back and see my journey was one of self-discovery on behalf of well-being.

Clearly, I was initially seeking well-being for myself.

Up until the training, I thought that this journey was about discovering who David was. What would make him happy? What could he do in life to make enough money to survive or even thrive? What kind of partner would David need in life to be happily married?

I was pretty good at undertaking this journey. I even got a PhD to legitimize this exploration.

My experience with meditation merely opened up the realm of self beyond my identity as David. The notion of cosmic consciousness, introduced by the Maharishi Mahesh Yogi, suggested I was intimately connected to, even a part of, a much larger self that included everything and everyone. (In Eckhart Tolle's book *A New Earth, Awakening to Your Life's Purpose,* he refers to this notion as the divine life essence.[1])

Now it was all coming together. My past was perfect and had prepared me for the future. I had done an incredible amount of research on how human beings act, think, and feel about their lives. I could clearly see how one's identity was a necessary part of one's existence. Yet I could also see how it was a trap. While it served as our piece on the game board of life, it also maintained the illusion that I am an individual, separate from others. This illusion dooms us to a life in which we ultimately do not feel connected to others, to the planet, to our self—the universal self.

So the theme that continuously expresses itself in my life is providing well-being for human beings.

Over time, I played with many forms for maximizing my effectiveness and impact. Because I discovered so much of this in the EST training (later Landmark), I worked for EST for several years, developing myself and learning and leading their programs.

In 1994, I started the Transitions Institute, which embodied my previous education in psychology, extensive engagement in meditation, and experience at Landmark. At the Transitions Institute, I developed a set of programs to *give people access to themselves.*

---

1 Eckhart Tolle, *A New Earth: Awakening to Your Life's Purpose* (New York: Penguin, 2005).

To me, this is the key to providing well-being to others. The trick would be to reveal that an individual's "identity" was not the whole story and provide an experience where a person could step beyond identity, step outside of psychological paradigms, and discover the unlimited awesome nature of being human.

Eckhart Tolle wrote that any life form can undergo 'enlightenment' (or transformation).[2] It is, however, an extremely rare occurrence, since it is more than an evolutionary progression. It requires a leap to an entirely different level of being.

Tolle went on to ask some powerful questions of those considering such a transformation.

1. Are you ready for a transformation of consciousness?
2. Can we as human beings lose the density of our conditioned mind structures?
3. Can we defy the gravitational pull of materialism and materiality and rise above identification of form that keeps the ego in place and condemns us to be imprisoned within our own identities?

*I believe that I have accomplished this transformation
for myself.*

IF I CAN, YOU CAN

---

2   Tolle, *A New Earth.*

YOU CAN

TRANSFORMATION MADE EASY

2

SELF–DISCOVERY

This is not a self-improvement book. This book supports self-discovery.

Discovering what? Great question! Discovering a fundamental paradigm shift that can empower you to achieve higher levels of success and happiness.

Not so long ago, we humans experienced several significant paradigm shifts that completely altered life on planet Earth. First, approximately five hundred years ago, Copernicus "discovered" that Earth revolved around the sun, rather than the opposite. Also around that same time, Galileo almost lost his life to the Roman Inquisition for declaring that Earth was round, not flat. Both discoveries had a profound impact on all to follow. Both discoveries refined our view of our world and the galaxy that we live in. But notice that neither focuses on us or on our nature as human beings.

We remain quite the mystery to ourselves. Yes, we are learning much about how our bodies and brains function, but we are still in search of the WHYs and HOWs of human nature and behavior.

Over the last hundred years or so, psychology has led the way in our theorizing why people are the way they are and do what they to. But after more than a hundred years of research and treatment strategies, no one in their right mind would argue we understand or that our mental health system is making progress.

The futility of psychotherapy is obvious. While psychology has become a billion-dollar industry, the statistics are more than alarming:

- Drug abuse is rampant, among not only adults but also school-age children

- Alcoholism is at an all-time high and even the best recovery programs can't boast a 25 percent recovery rate

- Our prisons are bursting at the seams, with 85 percent of prisoners returning

- Teenage pregnancy and sexually transmitted diseases are epidemic

- More children are being identified as ADD or ADHD and are on medications

- The occurrence of autism is skyrocketing

- Marriages fail more than 50 percent of the time

- Less than 25 percent of all children in the United States grow up in a home with their natural parents

My intent is not to bash the current system but to tell the truth about it. It is not working! I want to offer a simple model that will guide you on an inner journey of self-discovery—one in which you will gain access to your true self and real power.

- If you are up to something really big,

- If you want to move up to the next level of success,

- If you are reaching for a better or more meaningful relationship,

- If you feel you have run the course in your career and are ready for what's next, then consider this:

The key to a great life is to recognize that you and I, as human beings, are creating our lives moment by moment.

True success and joy belong to those who master the art of creating their lives, not those who are getting better at changing their circumstances.

While we are already creating our lives, we are doing so without the slightest bit of recognition that we are doing it. We are so deeply and profoundly trying to change for the better, we completely miss the obvious.

We are creating our lives now, now, now.

Right now, you are having an experience of the paragraph that you just read. Are you aware that you just *created* that experience? Anyone other than you reading that same paragraph will have a different experience. Some fairly similar. Some completely different.

You are totally unique. You are the only one on planet Earth that experiences life exactly the way you do.

You need to understand why and how you create your experience and how others create theirs. Actually, a cool aspect of this is that when you understand why and how you generate and create YOU, you will instantly also understand how others create their experiences.

In the pages to follow, I will lay out the Transitions Process, which is designed to give you access to yourself.

3

INTRODUCTION TO TRANSITIONS

The Transitions Process is a powerful journey of self-discovery and freedom: freedom from one's past limitations and freedom to create an often unpredictable, extraordinary future.

Successful and happy people are literally living into a future that inspires, enlivens, and sustains them. Transitions are about having an intentional and committed relationship with your future.

THE DIFFERENCE BETWEEN CHANGE AND TRANSITIONS

Transitions is not just a fancy word for *change*. I define change as A to B, A to chair, A to anything other than A.

I define *transitions* as A to B, one to two, summer to fall, seed to flower. In other words, there is a natural, sequential, directional progression to a transition.

You can identify countless examples of transition in your own life, such as education. You started in grade school or even pre-

20

school and advanced through high school. For many of us, it's going on to college and perhaps graduate school and a professional degree.

You have experienced transition in relationships. You started by dating, then you went steady, then you got engaged and eventually married and perhaps had kids. For more than 50 percent of adults, the next transition, divorce, probably wasn't in the original plan. And then for many, on to the next marriage partner.

In your professional life, you started with an entry position and, hopefully, advanced up the organizational ladder.

You and I—and all human beings—are always in a state of transition. Your entire past, all your experiences, decisions, choices, and so forth have played a role in how you have transitioned to this point. Most transitions appear to be gradual, only becoming clear after time.

For a young person, the transition process is transparent. It's like air to the bird and water to the fish. It is occurring but not noticed. It's much easier to see it in retrospect than at the time it is occurring.

Chances are you didn't spend a great deal of time consciously designing how you transitioned into the person you now call *you*. While you had goals, hopes, intentions, and so forth, they were probably not organized and thought out as the road map to your future.

The Transitions Process is about having an *enlightened* relationship with your future. It's about having a high level of awareness and intention regarding where you are going in life. It's about identifying your commitments, strengths, and core values and having them intentionally guide your choices regarding your actions, your accomplishments, how to relate to others, and who you want to be.

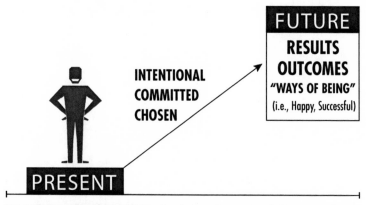

TRANSITIONS PROCESS: Having an Intentional, Committed, and Chosen Relationship with One's Future

A SHIFT IN PERSPECTIVE

Many of us would say we have a good life if asked. But if we are honest, we would also say that we live with an annoying sense that we should be happier, be more joyful. We go around with a feeling that something is missing or with distrust for how the future will unfold. Consider the examples below.

- Amy is a single mom of two and an attorney. She can't shake the feeling that she has no time to do the things she really wants to do. She feels like her life no longer belongs to her.

- Craig works for a start-up tech company and feels pressure to perform at ever-increasing levels of effectiveness.

- Phil is wondering if he retired too early. He's played lots of golf but longs to get back *in the game.*

- Chris is deeply concerned about the toll his professional success has had on his family.

Like the rest of us, they try their best to balance their responsibilities and their hopes and dreams. But the reality for most of us is that *we gotta work, we gotta raise a family*, and eventually the *good life* gets derailed by the simple process of living. Our lives seem to drift into a series of time, energy, and money traps. At first, the drift is subtle, unnoticed, dismissed, or excused as just part of *real life*, the price of having to make necessary compromises. But over time, we become accustomed to this relentless assault on our sense of well-being, joy, and happiness. We accept it as the new normal, and our conventional thinking tells us, "That's just the way it is; we are doing our best."

What if conventional thinking is just that? It leaves you with what's predictable, already known, and familiar.

Would you be willing to engage in a radically different way of relating to yourself? Would you be willing to discuss an entirely different relationship with your life, your self, your future?

REACHING FOR THE EXTRAORDINARY

For Mindy, an international art dealer and collector, life had become a blur—a million things coming at her at once.

"I started the Transitions Process with David based on a conversation with a friend that I trusted implicitly. He persuaded me to meet David while visiting New York on a business trip. So, I scheduled a session with Dr. Zelman. It turned out to be one of the most positive and intellectually challenging days I'd had in a long time. I didn't want it to end.

"David works with companies and individuals who have been highly successful in their businesses, but recognize they haven't gone as far as they can. In order to focus on the next giant leap, what I needed most was to organize and prioritize all my projects and commitments. David taught me to slow down, take stock, and focus on one thing at a time. He helped me make my path forward clear and attainable."

Frank, who runs an internationally renowned import/export business, knew he could be performing at a higher level professionally. He believed he was missing the keys to access an even higher income. Within a matter of months, the Transitions Process resulted in a major deal, lifting him far beyond his previous plateau.

"The process evolved in a magical way," he said. "I was able to visualize and live my future as if I had already won. I was able to put myself in the future and work from there. Amazing results!"

Lester Wunderman is known as the "father of direct marketing." He invented tear-out subscription cards in magazines and advertising inserts in Sunday newspapers, and helped turn the Columbia Record Club into one of the world's largest marketing organizations. But after a lifetime of accomplishment, while sitting as chairman of a major advertising agency, he faced a turning point: retirement or reentry into a second career. The Transitions Process helped him recognize his own untapped potential and redesign a future based on that potential.

"I came out of the session with this whole new theory on reengagement," Wunderman said. "Everybody can be employed, but few people can be engaged. David and I dealt with that. I got a better view of what it was that I wanted to do and what process I wanted to be involved with, which is to reassemble myself into another level. Thank goodness for this program. It shifted my perspective from retirement to reengagement."

Now it's your turn. Please take some time and complete the following questionnaire. The questions are designed to help you *intentionally* step into your future. The Transitions Process is about having an intentional, committed, and chosen relationship with your future. The better you are able to articulate a future of your own choosing, the easier it is to reach it.

THE TRANSITIONS PROCESS PRECOURSE QUESTIONNAIRE

1. Standing in the future—three to five years out—what would you want your life to look like in the following areas:

   - Family

   - Career

   - Lifestyle

   - Health

   - Wealth

   - Sense of purpose

   - Sense of freedom

   - Sense of accomplishment

2. Are there any circumstances, situations, or concerns that constrain or limit your view of what is possible in the future?

3. Is there anything you feel you need to fix, change, or address to maximize your sense of personal power?

4. If you increased your ability to influence others, whom would you choose to influence and regarding what?

5. If you increased your ability to resolve conflicts, which conflicts would you weigh in on?

6. If you were able to increase the odds of successfully fulfilling your next venture, what project would you take on?

7. What are your core values and core commitments?

8. Which of your attributes do you consider most important in achieving your personal and professional success?

If you have completed the precourse questionnaire, you should have a sense of what tangible results you want to accomplish. You may also have a sense of *whom you want to be.* Do you want to be more confident, more relaxed, more inspired, more passionate? Remember, the Transitions Process is about having an intentional committed relationship with a future of your choosing.

For Mindy, the future she was committed to was taking her business to the next level, and being more organized and focused in the process. For Phil, it was getting back in the game, feeling like he could still compete and excel in his profession.

Critical to their successes, and to all successes, is the need to take the actions that produce outcomes and results. Without the appropriate action, we seldom achieve our goals. Our actions lead us to succeed or fail.

So here are two critical questions: Why do people do what they do? Why do people take or not take a certain set of actions?

4

INTERNAL
CONVERSATIONS

THE KEY TO HUMAN BEHAVIOR

There are many theories on why people do what they do—or don't do—in life. According to Sigmund Freud, the ego (the action-oriented portion of the personality he believed made people do what they do) is stuck between the demands of society and the demands of instinct. This idea led him to develop psychoanalysis— the "talking cure"—a famous method of therapy in which patients use conversation to discover the hidden meanings of their actions.

On the other end of the spectrum, B. F. Skinner believed the science of psychology must rest exclusively on the idea that all behavior is learned. From his concept, he developed effective methods for observing and manipulating human actions.

The wide gulf between Freud's psychoanalytic and Skinner's behaviorist psychology is filled with a whole spectrum of other methods. Each one provides its own unique perspective on the influence of heredity versus the influence of experience. But the same dilemma resides in the heart of all psychologies: the science is far more adept at describing behavior and emotional conditions than it is at creating adaptability and giving people access to happiness and a sense of fulfillment in life.

A STARTLING DISCOVERY:
WHY PEOPLE DO WHAT THEY DO

I have made a simple yet profoundly powerful observation: human beings do what they do, not because of external forces or circumstances, but based on inner dialogues they are having with themselves. That's right. The lives that people live are the direct result of the inner dialogues taking place in their minds.

To make this point, I invite you into a college classroom with me. I'm about to have this very conversation with a group of students.

DZ   The question is, what's required for producing results? What do people have to do in order to produce results?

Student   *Work hard.*

DZ   Yeah, you have to work hard. Let me translate that into you have to take action. You okay with that? No action, no result. On the other hand, if you take action A, you get result A. You take action B, you get result B. Simple, isn't it?

Okay, here is where it gets really interesting. If results are a function of the actions that you take, what are your actions a function of? What's the source of your actions? Why do people do what they do 100 percent of the time?

Students   *Because they want something.*

Fear.

Because you're supposed to.

Need or desire.

Personality.

DZ   These are great answers but won't explain why we do what we do 100 percent of the time.

Students   *Motivation. We seek a reward.*

Because we learned in the past.

To get money.

DZ   I've asked hundreds, if not thousands, of groups the same question, and they come up with the same set of answers. Doesn't matter what country, what age group. Students, executives, athletes, professionals—all give the same answers. It's pretty interesting to me that we've had the study of psychology around for more than a hundred years, and psychologists are still theorizing on the source of the action instead of nailing it.

I need a volunteer. I request someone come up here and help me demonstrate what people's actions are correlated to 100 percent of the time. Tiffany, thanks for volunteering. We are going to demonstrate what your actions are correlated to. Would you take this please? (I'm holding out a pen for Tiffany to take, which she does.) Can I have it back? (Tiffany hands it back.) Now, why did you take it?

Tiffany   *Because you asked me to.*

DZ   That's what everybody says, because I asked you. (I present Tiffany with the same pen.) This is a live, poisonous rattlesnake. Take it please.

Tiffany   *No way!*

DZ   So, can you see that it's not because I asked you to, is
            it? Not really. I want you to see what's missing—and
            it's missing because it's so damn obvious. Your actions
            are perfectly correlated, but not to the conversation you
            are having with me. Your actions are a perfect match
            to the conversation you are having with yourself—your
            inner dialogue, your inner conversation. Your actions
            are always correlated to what you are telling yourself.

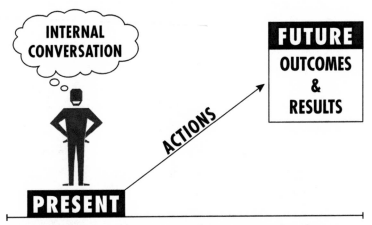

TRANSITIONS PROCESS: Internal Conversation Correlates to
One's Actions and Leads to
Outcomes and Results.

You're orchestrating what you do. No one else. Really! It often looks
like it's a function of your circumstances. It looks like someone else
is telling you what to do. But if you actually look, if you examine it,
you will see that you are always the one telling yourself what to do.

      You are the one telling yourself to get out of bed or hit the snooze
alarm. You're telling yourself what and when to eat. You are the one
telling yourself to run another mile or try to go faster. Whatever

you do—or don't do—you are the source of your behavior. This may sound insignificant. It's not. If you could actually get the relationship between your thoughts and your mind/body connection, you could start dictating a whole new set of conversations.

Whenever you notice the conversations you are currently engaged in do not lead to the outcome you desire, you can simply create a new conversation that does lead to a future of your choosing.

Here are some interesting aspects related to the internal conversation:

- Your internal conversation is unique to you. There are seven billion people on planet Earth. No one else is having the same internal conversation you are having.

- While we sometimes think we know what another person is thinking, for the most part, we don't. Therefore, others seldom know what you are thinking. If you want someone to know what you are thinking, tell them.

- Conversations require both speaking and listening. Two people speaking and no one listening is not a conversation. That's like having two speakers hooked up to separate stereos playing different records in the same room. Lots of noise, but no conversation.

- You don't *run* your internal conversation. It's on automatic. It plays 24-7 every day of your life. You can't turn it off. If you don't believe me, tell it to be silent and see how that goes.

- Since it is always running, if I say something to you, I am actually interrupting it.

- When another person is speaking, we often don't do a good job of distinguishing what the other person is saying versus our interpretation of what they are saying. That's how fast our internal conversation is processing what is being said.

- It is uncommon for others to simply hear what you say. If you are a CEO speaking to your executive team of five people, and you tell them that you are slashing the price of an existing product you sell, each person at the table is hearing something different. Sales hears, "Great. More demand, but I'll have to sell more units to make my financial commitment." Customer service hears, "Better staff up for additional client base." And production hears, "How the hell are we going to meet the demand? We are already running at capacity."

  If you are having a family discussion around the dinner table, and you tell your husband and kids you want to go to your brother's house for spring break, just notice their reactions. Your teenage daughter is devastated, because she wanted to hang out with her boyfriend. Your ten-year-old son is happy, because he gets to play with his cousin. And your husband is trying to figure out whether it's better to fly or drive.

  The point is, if you say something to five people, you are actually having five different conversations.

- I've saved the best for last. Your actions correlate to your internal conversations, and so do your emotions, feelings, moods, attitudes, point of view, beliefs, and so forth. When you get a notice from the bank that says one of the checks you deposited came back for insufficient funds, you are likely to feel confusion or anger or just be upset. When a police car pulls behind you with its lights flashing, you might have a thought like, "Oh, s**t! What did I do wrong?" Bet you also experience a bit of fear or concern. When you close a deal and the check gets deposited in the bank, you might think,

"Yay! We did it!" And guess what? You also feel great. You have a sense of accomplishment.

Taking several of these observations together, we can say that your personal reality (mood, attitude, feelings, emotions, point of view, belief, and actions) is directly related to the internal conversation occurring for you at any moment.

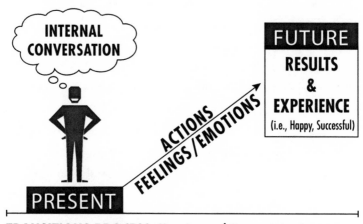

TRANSITIONS PROCESS: Your Internal Conversation is Also a Perfect Match for Your Feelings, Emotions, Etc.

There are two very important implications from this discussion:

1. Since you are the only one on planet Earth with your unique set of internal conversations, you are the only one who can be responsible for them. It doesn't help to blame others or the circumstances. Only you can change your conversation.

2. Here is the really good news: *Conversations are only conversations.* They can be changed; in fact, you change conversa-

tions all the time. You don't want to see a particular movie. Then a friend says they saw it and loved it. You change your "mind" and decide you will see it. You were angry with someone and then decided to get over it. And so on.

A NOTE OF CAUTION

Simply changing the conversation and taking certain actions does not guarantee a result. Sure, you changed your internal conversation from "I'm not going to apply for that position because they'll never select me" to "I'm going to submit my application, because I am committed to getting that job." This does not ensure you will get the job, but by applying, you have dramatically altered your chance of succeeding.

THE TRANSITIONS MODEL IS A VERY SIMPLE MODEL.

If it sounds confusing or difficult to comprehend, perhaps it's because of all the internal conversations you are listening to. Simply put, the results you produce are a function of the actions you take, and the actions you take are directly correlated to your internal conversation.

5
AUTOMATIC CONVERSATIONS

The quality of one's life at any moment is directly correlated to the internal conversation currently occurring. Since you can't change anything you can't see or hear, becoming aware of these internal *background* conversations is an important first step.

TWO PRIMARY TYPES OF INTERNAL CONVERSATIONS

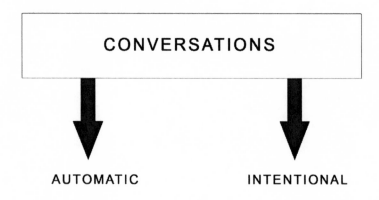

CONVERSATIONS

AUTOMATIC   INTENTIONAL

AUTOMATIC CONVERSATIONS ARE DESIGNED FOR OUR SURVIVAL

Internal conversations are natural. We all have them. Not surprisingly, they seem to reflect our past experiences and learning. The conversations that we are referring to as *automatic* seem to be built in. Their purpose appears to be to protect us from danger, both physical and emotional. If we are in the street and the bus is coming, it's not in our survival interest to have to figure out what to do. The automatic conversation is, "Get out of the way. Now!"

Another quality of automatic conversations is they are *already always there*. Think about it. You don't wake up and turn on your brain in the morning. Even if you are feeling sluggish when you first open your eyes, you're already in the midst of many conversations, ranging from "I need coffee" to "I've got to get to work" to "What am I going to wear today?" as well as "Why didn't I hear from him or her yesterday?"

It seems as though the internal conversation runs continuously 24-7. At night, when you put your head down on the pillow, the voice in your head is often very loud, assessing how the day went, what we should have done, what made us happy, and so forth. In other words, it has something to say about everything. Eventually you pass out, but the voice keeps talking, keeps processing. Sometimes, it even speaks to us when we are sleeping in the form of dreams.

SIX EXAMPLES OF AUTOMATIC CONVERSATIONS

1. Judgments

Human beings are judgment / assessment machines. We judge everything and everyone, including ourselves. We assess our relationships, our homes, our jobs, the weather, and someone's appearance. Even if someone says, "I love you," we judge whether they mean it.

We all listen through our own filters. We judge, evaluate, and take sides based on our histories and experiences. These assessments or judgments are more often than not negative rather than positive. While the majority of these assessments are not "The sky is falling" or "Everything sucks," very few sound like, "This is perfect!" or "You are the best thing that ever happened to me."

If you could rate all your internal conversations on a scale somewhere between 1 and 10, few would measure up to your standards. It is my experience that most of us are getting along, rather than killing it. If you tell the truth, you might see many things about yourself that do not meet your own standards—what you should or shouldn't eat, how you exercise, the time you spend with your family, or taking care of your kids or the car. These assessments take up a great deal of our mental and emotional bandwidths and have a direct effect on how we get to *be* right now.

Do you want to know why you are the way you are? It's because you are the product of the sum of all the conversations you have ever had, plus the ones that are occurring right now! How you *be* on a daily basis is a reflection of which conversations have airtime.

One of the biggest mistakes people make is to try to *stop these conversations*. It's not an easy thing to do. As you will see shortly, I suggest that rather than trying to stop or change these conversations, simply generate an alternative conversation to take the place of the existing one.

We all know that two objects can't occur in the same place at the same time. That is, if I had two bricks, one in each hand, and I tried to force them into the same space at the same time, it would be impossible. So, too, is it that you can't have two separate and different conversations at the same time. Yes, you can change back and forth very rapidly between yes and no, but you can't be saying yes if you are saying no. Therefore, the most efficient way of not having a particular conversation is to *create a new conversation* to take its place. "I don't have time to go to the gym" can be replaced with, "After I exercise I'm energized and can get more done."

Remember, judgments / assessments and other automatic conversations are not bad or wrong. They are *just* conversations.

2. Personal Conversations

Personal conversations sound a lot like:

> *I want . . .*
> *I need . . .*
> *I think . . .*
> *My opinion is . . .*
> *My feelings . . .*
> *My day off . . .*

These conversations place you at the center of the discussion, whether it is an internal conversation or one you are having with others. Once again, without these *I-based* conversations, you wouldn't survive. You have to attend to your needs. However, I think you would agree that it gets real old very fast when people are concerned only with themselves. It is not much fun hanging with them when they are focused only on themselves and turn every conversation into something about them. People extremely focused on themselves find it difficult to engage in meaningful relationships, both personally and professionally.

3. Looking Good

We all—at least most of us—want to look good in the eyes of others. Whether it's our parents, friends, teachers, or even just acquaintances, we try to impress others, to be liked, and to be well thought of.

There is a cost to always trying to look good. People don't say what they think for fear of offending. All too often in a relationship, people talk about the weather or what's on TV because they avoid the *tough* conversations. When we are trying to *make it* with someone, to be accepted or fit in, we often say and do what we think others expect us to say or do. But when we are doing this, we are being inauthentic, and the lack of authenticity costs you your power.

I love the Oscar Wilde quote, "Be yourself; everyone else is already taken."

4. Application

This is the "how" conversation. How can I use this? How are we going to do this? How are we going to get it done? How am I going to find the time? How can we get it done faster, cheaper? How can I get her to like me? How can I lose weight?

When I'm leading the Transitions Process, the most frequent form this conversation takes is: *How* can I use what I'm learning? *How* can I apply this information in my job or relationship?

These sound like great questions. After all, they are *use-full*. But carried to an extreme, this frame of mind often manifests itself as impatience, being distracted, and a lack of appreciation or not being fully present. It sounds like, *Hurry up. Give me the answer. Don't waste my time. This isn't good enough. I'm not good enough. I have to keep pressing forward. I have to get my to-do list done. Faster.*

It's not uncommon for people to feel like they are being run by the things they have to do and that no matter what, you *coulda, shoulda* done better.

5. Being Right

When you are in an argument with someone, who is right and who is wrong? Has it ever been the case you discovered you were, in fact, the one who was wrong? Please notice that you were absolutely right . . . until the moment you weren't. Being right is a frame of mind where you are absolutely right; therefore, there is no need for further discussion.

In our thoughts, things *are* a particular way, and there is no opportunity for you to question or relinquish your beliefs. For example: "You know how Dad is. He's domineering and controlling. He always has to get his way." These observations live as fact, not a conversation—not as a point of view.

Other expressions of being right are:

- My way or the highway.
- I already know, so why should I ask?
- I'm certain I'm right, and you're wrong.
- Tell me what you think. Uh-huh. Now let me set you straight.

We speak through these filters, and we listen through them as well. We listen to others from a preconceived notion, saying, "I'm right. They're wrong. If they are unwilling to see it my way, that's their problem."

6. Resignation

Last, but certainly not least, we have the filter we call *resigna-*

tion. It is the glue that holds all the other filters in place. Resignation sounds like this:

- That's the way it is. You can't change it, him, or them.
- You can't fight City Hall.
- You know the way I am.
- Accept me the way I am because I can't change.
- I can't [fill in the blank]—ride a horse, go to college, earn a decent living, make the sale, get through to my kids.
- I'd like to take a vacation, but I have too much work.

When people feel stuck, there is no way out and nothing they can do. That's resignation.

6
INTENTIONAL CONVERSATIONS

We must generate conversations *for* the future. They're not automatic. Just as automatic, past-based conversations guide our actions, so too do intentional future-based conversations. However, there is an important distinction between the two. Future-based conversations generate actions toward the possibility of fulfilling our commitments and intentions. They open possible futures rather than automatically shut them out. They provide a clear, direct way of accessing your personal power and designing your future.

Here are several important factors regarding intentional conversations:

- They are *for* the future.

- They transform identity-based psychological conversations into committed self-expressions.

- They reflect our core wiring and core values. All humans, all cultures, share these values.

- They are always available, just not as obvious, because they are initially displaced by automatic conversations.

- To access intentional conversations, you often have to catch yourself in an automatic conversation and *intentionally* switch.

- Intentional conversations provide growth, learning, and most important, *creating your future.*

- This simple set of six intentional conversations can provide a reliable go-to place to stand for generating yourself as a match for any future you are committed to creating.

- This set of conversations is like a menu. Choose any one to displace an automatic conversation.

- I call these conversations tools. Tools to presence oneself to *be present,* they all have the power to call forth a future rather than describe something from the past.

- Bottom line: intentional conversations create, generate, and invent a new reality, right now! They have the power to transform your relationship with yourself, others, and any circumstances, right now!

In the previous chapter, six examples of automatic conversations were offered. Now contrast them with the six examples of intentional conversations:

Automatic versus Intentional Conversations	
AUTOMATIC	**INTENTIONAL**
Status quo, already set, always there, history, past-based, stingy	Future-based, created, chosen experience, generous, break-through
JUDGMENTS Judge others and self; limits; standards and shoulds	COMMITMENTS What is the commitment in the background? What are they committed to?
PERSONAL I-based; what's in it for me?	PARTNERSHIP We-based; community; empowerment
LOOKING GOOD Compromise; conform	BELONGING Vulnerable; risk
APPLICATION How can I use this? What's it good for?	CONTRIBUTION Value
BEING RIGHT I'm right, you're wrong; I already know . . .	OPEN Inclusive; put aside my point of view to hear yours
RESIGNATION No possibility; "is" world—it is that way	POSSIBILITY Creative; allowing for another way/idea

Each of the six intentional conversations corresponds directly across to an automatic conversation. While the best way of shifting an assessment is with a commitment, any one of the intentional conversations can replace any one of the automatic conversations.

SIX EXAMPLES OF INTENTIONAL CONVERSATIONS

1. Commitment

All human beings are 100 percent committed 100 percent of the time. The only question is, what am I being committed to right now?

We are often pulled in several directions by competing commitments. "I want to go out and meet my friends, but I have to study for the test," or, "I really want to eat that dessert, but I'm trying to lose weight."

Here's the thing about commitments: you get to say what you are committed to. They live in our conversations. You have the power to declare who you are and who you will be under any circumstance, at any time. It is like a muscle that needs to be developed. The question is, can you be committed to train yourself to speak and listen committedly?

The key here is to speak and listen *for* commitments, to speak and listen on behalf of what you are committed to.

Stephen Covey said in his book, *The 7 Habits of Highly Effective People,* that the first habit is to "start with the end in mind." In other words, what are you out to accomplish? What future are you building? What are you committed to?[3]

WHATEVER YOU ARE COMMITTED TO SHAPES THE FUTURE.

When you are committed to a particular future, it is more likely to occur. If you are committed to your marriage, then it has a higher probability of succeeding than if you are not committed to

---

3   Stephen Covey, *The 7 Habits of Highly Effective People* (New York: Simon & Schuster, 2004).

it. One of the more frequent questions I'm asked is, if there is one thing that you can point to that explains your thirty-five years of a successful marriage, what is it? My response is that it's entering a marriage when you are committed to going the distance. I think many people say, "I do" aloud but secretly listen to that inner voice that says, "*Unless . . .*"

To be fully committed, you must listen rigorously to your internal conversation. Listen carefully to what you are telling yourself. If you do, you will have a much better handle on what you are committed to. That doesn't mean you won't have thoughts that seem to question your commitment or ability, but listen to how you respond to those disparaging conversations.

For example, after committing to running a marathon, it is natural to have thoughts like: "But what if I can't train as effectively as I plan?" or "What if I don't lose the twenty pounds I need to prior to the race?" If your next thought is, "I don't care about what-ifs. I'm running the race," then you are probably going to be okay. You can't just commit to something once. Committing requires you recommitting and recommitting.

While it takes some practice, I know each of us is capable of discerning whether a conversation is intentionally committed or not. "I'll pay you back" or "Let's get together for lunch sometime" are examples of what someone who lacks commitment might say. Compare that with, "I get paid at the end of month, so I'll bring you a check on the first," or "I am free for lunch next Thursday. Can you join me?"

2. Partnership

We all know a true partnership is neither simple nor easy. I developed and led a course called "The Partners' Retreat" in which couples take three days to explore their partnerships. One of the more fascinating aspects of partnership is that we must often *surrender* our individuality on behalf of a larger possibility of *being* partners. When two individuals get married and say, "I do," in that moment they each declare themselves as responsible for the marriage rather than just being responsible for themselves. I often say it's hard for me to be really happy if my wife is unhappy. Others say it a little differently: happy wife, happy life. Without going into a deep discussion on partnership right now, suffice to say that partnership is about we, us, win–win.

In an earlier incarnation, I had a business partner, Kathi, who taught me, actually trained me, in the art of partnership. She ruthlessly demanded to be listened to and spoken to so that every conversation mattered. There were no throwaway conversations. The breakthrough I had with Kathi was the discovery that as a partner, I had to be just as committed to Kathi reaching her goals as I was to me reaching mine. It wouldn't work for one of us to feel fulfilled if the other was left hanging.

Without a doubt, my best partner in life is my wife, Karen. Her ability to see the bigger picture, to stand for what we can accomplish together, is amazing. I am truly blessed to have a life partner that loves me unconditionally. Once again, I have to say that it's not simple, not easy. But both of us are committed to spending our lives together, and we are always standing for each other's success.

I often say to my clients, "If my arm is broken, I get it fixed. Why? Because I'm going to need that arm to live fully." The same thing in marriage. We are partners for life. If we have a problem in our marriage, we get it fixed. Don't blame your arm for being broken. That won't resolve anything.

3. Belonging

Perhaps the most prevalent missing conversation is one of

belonging, a feeling of ownership, a sense of "I am part of this family, company, or community. I belong." I don't have to make it or fake it to fit in or prove anything to anyone.

As I am writing this, I'm sitting in my lake house in Gunbarrel, Texas. I am totally at home. This is my home. I belong. If I were sitting in my best friend's home out here on the lake, it would feel different. When you belong, there isn't a whole lot of background noise, rationalizing, or figuring out what to do. You just act as an expression of yourself. Belonging is a gift you grant to yourself.

4. Contribution

Give people a chance to contribute, and they will perform at an extraordinary level. Take away the opportunity to contribute, and people will just go through the motions because they believe their actions won't make any real difference. It seems as though everyone wants to make a difference, to contribute in some way to their friends, family, organization, and so forth. We are always looking for ways to use our talents and gifts to make our unique contribution. But interestingly, we often resist others making a contribution to us.

In the following discussion with a client named Ken, a movie mogul in California, he expressed his discomfort with being contributed to by others:

DZ Do you want to contribute to people?

Ken *Yeah, of course!*

DZ How about you? Do you want to be contributed to?

Ken *Definitely not!*

DZ What's that about?

Ken	*Well, in general, no, because it's an attack.*
DZ	It is?
Ken	*Definitely! I mean, sometimes I think it's really great, and I want their help. But most of the time, it feels like they are sticking their nose in my business, and they don't know what they are talking about.*
DZ	But you do want to contribute to others?
Ken	*Definitely. But if I didn't have something to contribute to someone, I wouldn't force it.*

It's interesting how Ken relates to contribution as an attack. If he is experiencing an attack, then what he's receiving certainly isn't being received as a contribution. I think that at one time, I saw things the same way as Ken sees them. For a long time I interpreted my father's interactions with me as an attack in the form of domination and control. For years, I did everything I could to avoid or resist him. When my son, Michael, was born, my father wanted to spend lots of time with his new grandson; I had a concern. He screwed me up with his domination and control crap, and I didn't want him ruining my kids. But I did want him to have time with his grandson. I couldn't possibly see not allowing that.

So I went to a colleague of mine and said, "I've got to shift this conversation." I knew that if I were going to create a new conversation, it had to be authentic. I couldn't just make something up. You actually have to believe it. I couldn't think of anything, so I started to examine my relationship with my son. I saw there was never a day in my life that I woke up wanting to dominate or control Michael. Then I started questioning whether my father was actually trying to dominate and control me.

I admit to being confused at first. So I asked myself, What do I want in my relationship with Michael? There were only two things. I wanted to always be able to participate and to contribute. That's all I wanted! If I could participate in his life and contribute to him, I'd be happy. I think that's the basis of a great relationship: participating and contributing.

Then it struck me. Dominate and control could look a lot like participate and contribute. I realized that I had been reacting to the form rather than the substance of my interactions with my father. So I called him and said, "Hey, Dad. I'm going to start relating to you as a huge contribution in my life."

From that point on, I held him as a contribution, and our relationship completely transformed. My dad became my best friend . . . again. As long as you are relating to people's attempts to contribute as an attack, it's not going to go well. The unfortunate part is that if your filter for being contributed to is very small, almost nothing done on your behalf can be experienced as a contribution.

Be open to others who are trying to contribute to you. In reality, it's a lot easier to achieve the things you want in life if you allow others to play a role.

5. Open and Honest

Much if not all of our personal experience, including our beliefs, perceptions, feelings, and so forth, are directly correlated to our internal conversations.

Can you hear what you are telling yourself? That's your world, your reality! If you are telling yourself you are bored, you are. If you are telling yourself you are tired, you are. If your mind is saying you're thrilled with your work product, you are. But one must be aware that there is a whole world occurring "out there" and not "in here" in your mind.

If you are going to be a participant in life rather than an observer, you must listen keenly for how things, including you, are occurring for others. Don't immediately disagree or resist another's point of view. It's probably real for them. At the end of the day, you will select which conversations you choose to get "airtime." But initially, be open and include others' realities. This will make you a much wiser person.

6. Possibility

I want to start with the lens being open as wide as I can possibly get it. Human beings are the *possibility of possibility*.

There, now you have it. Human beings are the space where possibility occurs. No human beings, no possibility. Interestingly, human beings do not have a powerful relationship with possibility. Perhaps this is because we liken creativity and possibility to human traits, something we are born with, rather than it being natural to continually create possibilities.

None of us knows the future, but we do know that it will look different from the past or even the present. Change is a constant. Possibility could be thought of as the opportunity to say a future and then fulfill it.

Possibility is so exciting! All creative acts begin as possibilities. Then they mature into structured ideas upon which we can take action and realize the possibility. Before I could transform my relationship with my father, I had to see the possibility that I could accomplish it.

Anything you are putting up with, anything you are resigned to, can be shifted to a desired possible future.

7

SELF-ACCEPTANCE

It's very important that I clarify what I mean by self-acceptance. Typically self-acceptance is discussed in a psychological context, referring to an individual's strengths and weaknesses and that individual's relationship with their strengths and weaknesses. Obviously, you can't be great at everything, so it is often suggested that you identify your strengths and capitalize on them while mitigating your weaknesses as much as possible.

In the Transitions Process, self-acceptance is grounded in the recognition that human beings are infinitely more capable of performing at higher intellectual, emotional, and physical levels.

In fact, fifty years from now people will look back at our current capabilities and capacities and think of us much the same way as we think of others prior to the Industrial Revolution.

Self-acceptance requires accepting ourselves as vessels for the extraordinary. Human beings are the *opportunity* for intelligence to express itself on planet Earth. The speed of an individual's

53

transformation depends in part on what Carol Dweck refers to as "mindsets." She distinguishes between two fundamental mindsets: fixed and growth.[4]

FIXED MINDSET

The fixed mindset sees the way things currently are and embraces the current reality as the *right* reality. The brain's job is to make the most of what is currently understood. Change is a threat and should be avoided. Continuity, consistency, and the status quo should be maintained at all times.

GROWTH MINDSET

The growth mindset views every experience as an opportunity for learning. Every event informs us as to how we can improve. Our traits are just a starting point for development. The growth mindset is based on the notion that your basic qualities can be cultivated through effort.

Self-acceptance is not merely accepting what is but accepting oneself as an extraordinary, limitless potential.

As you can see, Dweck's fixed versus growth mindset paradigm is almost an exact mirror of the Transitions Program's Automatic and Intentional Conversations. One significant difference, however, is that Dweck is focused on the characteristics or results of one's internal conversations rather than the conversations themselves. Therefore, she provides a *macro* view. She then suggests that the mindset allows for certain actions and orientations based on whether one has a fixed or growth mindset.

Seems like chicken or the egg. I maintain that a mindset is composed of many individual conversations, and therefore the conversation is the causative agent.

---

4 Carol Dweck, *Mindset: The New Psychology of Success* (New York: Random House, 2006).

Once again, this is extremely important, because it is infinitely simpler to change a conversation than to change a mindset. As a matter of fact, I will argue that the only way to change a mindset *is* to change the conversation.

FUNDAMENTAL DIFFERENCES BETWEEN AUTOMATIC AND INTENTIONAL CONVERSATIONS

After seeing the following list of differences, you will be able to make a choice—not an either/or choice, but a choice regarding your preference. Do you wish to be grounded in and determined by automatic conversations or by intentional conversations? A similar question is, would you prefer to engage in life with a fixed mindset or a growth mindset?

I believe you have a choice!

If you choose to embrace intentional conversations and a growth mindset, your personal transformation will accelerate. You will be stepping into the possibility of being human—the excitement of being your own *creative designer!*

Automatic/Fixed	Intentional/Growth
1. Focused on the past	1. Focused on the future
2. Focused on what already is	2. Focused on what could be
3. Focused on survival	3. Focused on achievement
4. Designed to reduce risk-taking	4. Embraces risk as necessary for learning
5. One's identity and role in life are relatively fixed	5. One's character and self-expression are a work in progress
6. It's important to understand and be right	6. It's important to push beyond the limits of what we know

Automatic/Fixed	Intentional/Growth
7. Point to the circumstances to explain the reason for their actions	7. Takes personal responsibility for their actions
8. Sees commitment as a constraint	8. Sees commitment as a tool for accomplishment
9. I am my feelings and thoughts	9. I have feelings and thoughts
10. I am my identity	10. I am an expression of myself

SEVERAL FUNDAMENTAL DIFFERENCES

Each time you choose an intentional conversation over an automatic one, you are planting a seed for your liberation. Over time, these seeds bloom, and a radiant, beautiful garden appears.

Complete and permanent self-acceptance may not occur with your first act of choosing, but each time you choose, you strengthen your awareness and consciousness that you have a choice.

> The key is to know that you are always at choice. You are the chooser.
>
> The moment you forget this, everything becomes hard and complicated.
>
> You have the right to choose. Now, exercise your right.

8

STINGY VS. GENEROUS CONVERSATIONS

Another term I use to describe automatic conversations is "stingy conversations." Conversely, intentional conversations are referred to as "generous conversations."

Why stingy? Because this set of conversations leaves you with, at best, what you already have: your judgments and assessments, what you already *know* from experience, and, of course, resignation—the certainty that you can't do anything to make things better.

Generous conversations are *for the future*. They are all about growth, learning, and an expanded sense of self and possibility.

> Shifting from stingy to generous conversations is one of the most empowering acts of self-expression and transformation we can engage in.

Below are a few examples in which my clients were able to identify their stingy conversations and switch.

Anthony, one of my wealthiest clients, said, "I'm depressed. I used to be on the front page of the *Wall Street Journal*, above the crease, and now I'm lucky if I'm mentioned on page 8. I now sit around a table talking deals worth several millions, rather than billions. I get the sense the younger guys are wondering, 'Why is he here?' And you know what? So am I!"

After a bit of dialogue, I suggested the following: "Anthony, it's clear to me, and everyone who knows you, that you have already won the game. You are thought of as one of the most success-ful business people of this era. The problem is, *you* haven't given yourself credit for what you have achieved. You're still out there on the field running plays long after the lights have gone off and all the fans have left the stadium. You are still trying to prove you can win a game you already won. Can you celebrate your accomplish-ments?"

Anthony got the message and created a very generous con-versation for himself. He threw himself a huge retirement party (to declare victory publicly) and then left to hike the Himalayas with his wife for six months. When he returned, he set up a new company supporting the creation of twenty-first-century infra-structure in third-world countries. Not surprisingly, several of his ventures are back in the billion-dollar range.

Lester Wunderman, as discussed earlier, came to me shortly after his board of directors asked him to step down as acting CEO. They wanted him to play a nonoperating role as chairman of the board emeritus. Lester was eighty years old at the time, and accord-ing to him, "No one wants to listen to me anymore. They want me to retire to a corner office and enjoy my remaining years. It feels like I've been sent to work in a soup kitchen."

In response to not being wanted on the front lines by his company, he began to question whether anything he had ever done really made a difference. During our conversation, Lester gave up his stingy self-assessment and acknowledged that the body of his work during his lifetime had made a huge contribution to the company, as well as to the advertising industry as a whole. He also realized that while he no longer had a job at Wunderman Inc., he didn't have to retire.

Once freed from his stingy conversation, there was a shift in his body language, in his tone; and there was that amazing twinkling in his eyes as he declared: "The choice is not whether to retire or not. The opportunity is to reengage. There are so many things that I can do, that I want to do, that I will now have the time to engage in. One of the first things on my list is to write another book on the topic of reengagement."

Lester has since published several books, been on the boards of several companies, and frequently exhibits an extraordinary collection of photographs he has taken. To sum it up, Lester said, "Everyone, including myself, thought it was time for me to retire. Thank goodness I learned to shift my perspective from retirement to reengagement."

Bruce, a very successful clothier, asked me to work with his daughter. He was very disappointed in her. She was a twenty-one-year-old college student getting very average grades from a very average university. When I met with Lisa, I asked her, "Do you know why we're talking?"

She replied, "Yes, because my father says I'm lazy. I hang out at my apartment, never go out, never study, and have no ambition."

I said, "It doesn't seem like you are lazy, but rather quite clever and powerful. You don't go out and get drunk. You don't do drugs. You have resisted many bad things that come from being one of the wealthiest kids on campus. You were wise to cloister yourself."

After a long discussion, she acknowledged that it was indeed hard to stay out of trouble, but she had done a good job of that. She also said that school was boring. When I asked her if anything interested her, she said she had a passion for fashion.

Nine months later, she graduated college. Eighteen months after that, Lisa started her own cashmere import business, which did more than $500,000 the first year!

I love this next story. Several years ago, my wife, Karen, and I went on a trip to India with a group of medical professionals and their spouses. On the trip, one of the physicians who participated fully in all our tour activities wouldn't climb the steps of a temple's steeple. Rick explained he had a fear of heights. Several days later, we were traveling together in a car, driven by a professional driver. The car was climbing up a small mountain range on a wide road, not even close to the drop-off. Once again, the physician became extremely agitated and said he had a fear of heights.

The following day was the last the group would be together. Knowing that I was a transitions coach, he approached me and asked if I knew of anything he could do to overcome his fear.

So I reminded him that we had spent the last fourteen days together with this amazing, accomplished group of men and women. We had all been exposed to many stressful if not danger-ous situations, not the least of which had been the daily drives in horrific traffic. We unexpectedly came upon snakes, not knowing if they were poisonous or not. We were all jarred, pushed, and crushed by untold thousands of people with their hands out and had hands laid on us, seeking a handout. Never once did I notice him lose his composure or confidence. But this thing about heights, when we were in no real danger, rattled him to the bone. Here is how and why I think that works.

Thoughts are like clouds. Clouds cross the sky and quickly disappear. Most of our thoughts do the same. Occasionally you see a cloud that grabs your attention. It may be moving quickly or resemble a dog or bird, or perhaps it's a brilliant color. Thoughts cross our minds and for the most part also quickly disappear. It's often hard to recall what we were thinking two minutes ago. Rather than just *having* a thought, we pay attention to it, and then we have another thought about the thought we just had.

Sometimes the second thought moves from an observation to a decision: "My uncle was playing with me, bouncing me around, and I fell off his shoulders and hurt myself." Falling hurts (observation). Then the decision: "I never want to fall and hurt myself again." Being up high increases the danger of falling. "I never want to be up high again." Or, "My best friend leaned out a window, fell, and broke his leg (observation). I never want that to happen to me (decision)."

While we make an untold number of observations on a daily basis, the decisions we make in response determine our experience. That decision not to get hurt by falling was a valuable decision to make at age three or four. However, you internalized it and gave it a very prominent role in determining your future experience. Since you are still here, we can assume that the conversation (don't put yourself in a situation where you fall and hurt yourself) has served you well.

But you know what? It's time to thank it and let it go so it can help other four-year-olds. You mastered the lesson and no longer need to carry that conversation with you.

I'd love to tell you that six months later I received a letter from Rick thanking me for our short and brilliant conversation, and that he is freed from his fear of heights. The truth is, I never heard from him again. What I can tell you is that I have reversed and completely transformed people's fears countless times by just inventing and creating a reasonable explanation that requires no additional mental churning. By making up a possible interpretation that doesn't require fixing anything or changing anything, we can just *let it go*.

Rick's opportunity is simply to choose any empowering story or interpretation and make it his own. (By the way, I'm also not suggesting that Rick and I walk over to some ledge and test my interpretation. He can still choose to avoid certain situations if they are uncomfortable. But I want the forty-six-year-old world-class physician choosing, not the four-year-old.)

On the road to freedom, you will certainly begin to notice how unfree you have been, and in many ways still are. Hundreds of historical commitments, habits, and distortions, both large and small, reveal themselves. They may appear as energy traps, places you get stuck or lose power.

Fortunately, as we now know, feelings of denial, anger, procrastination, victimhood, and so forth are only conversations. The key is to move quickly through less productive ones and shift to more purposeful ones. Our sense of freedom and joy in life directly correlates to taking responsibility for the very things we have been concerned about. It is equally important to focus on the future, and to focus on your commitments, visions, and dreams.

9

TAKING CHARGE

Taking charge of your life begins with the awareness that you have a choice regarding how you act and feel.

Most people can wrap their heads around the notion that they have a choice regarding their actions. They can clearly see they have a choice to get up and get to work on time or hit the snooze button. *News flash!* You also have a choice regarding how you feel.

Here's the key. We *have* feelings rather than we *are* our feelings. The same is true regarding our thoughts. We *have* thoughts rather than we *are* our thoughts. (More on this later.)

ABOUT YOUR FEELINGS

Let me say this again. I *have* feelings. I am *not* my feelings. Check out the difference:

I AM afraid of takings tests versus I HAVE a fear of test taking.

I AM afraid to ask her out versus I HAVE a fear of asking her out.

I AM stupid versus I FEEL stupid.

I AM depressed versus I HAVE feelings of depression.

Notice that we are not invalidating or trying to change the emotions. In both cases, we are acknowledging the presence of a feeling or an emotion.

In each statement, which begins with "I am" (afraid, stupid, depressed), I am saying that is *who I am*, which makes it a more permanent part of myself and, therefore, much more difficult to change.

In each of the corresponding second statements, I am referring to *my experience*, which by its very nature *will* change. Also, when I am *not* defined by my feelings or emotions, there's much I can do to alter how I feel.

We have a very strange relationship with our feelings. As human beings, we do a lot of *voting* on our feelings. Some are good and some are bad. Typically, people think that the following emotions and feelings are bad or wrong.

- Anger
- Hate
- Depression
- Confusion
- Inadequacy

Why can't we see that these feelings exist on a continuum? They are on the opposite end of a spectrum for something else:

Anger .... Pleasure

Hate .... Love

Sad .... Happy

Confused .... Certain

Inadequate .... Confident

I don't see how it is possible to have one of these emotions without the capacity for the other. God gave each of us a full range and set of emotions. All these emotions are a legitimate part of the human experience. It is our job to learn how to use them, to learn how to channel them into a productive life.

Do I have a preference? Of course I do. I would much rather be happy than sad, confident than fearful. But denying or resisting the feelings or experience I am having only causes more trouble.

It is important to allow yourself to *have* the feelings, to experience the feelings you are having. Having sadness when you are sad causes it to dissipate that much faster. In contrast, resisting your feelings or experiences causes them to persist. The same is true in an argument. The moment you *get* what the other person is saying, you acknowledge their feelings or point of view, and they no longer need to keep repeating their position. Resist their communication, and the argument continues.

The key is to realize that we *have* emotions and feelings. We are *not* our emotions and feelings. And, coming full circle, our emotions and feelings are merely (essentially) a product of our internal dialogues.

ABOUT YOUR THOUGHTS

Our thoughts play an instrumental role in determining our moment-by-moment reality. Unfortunately, many of our thoughts leave us in less-than-ideal circumstances.

Having unwanted thoughts is natural. Everyone has them. How you relate to them has everything to do with how well your life goes.

The whole notion that you can *control* your thoughts is problematic. That's why this chapter is "Taking Charge" rather than "Taking Control." Once you recognize a nonproductive conversation, you can shift it. But because so many of our conversations come from the past and are *automatic*, that is, they are in response to something that happened in the past, it is too late because they are already there!

If you can get to a place where you can recognize *a thought is just a thought*, not reality, then you can begin to reconstruct your thinking—or should I say change your *thought-ing*? Having a thought that "I'm afraid of roller coasters and shouldn't get on the ride" doesn't have to stop me. I can acknowledge my fear and generate another conversation: "What the heck? I'm going to get on anyway." After all, the first time most of us got on a roller coaster, we had plenty of second thoughts.

> A thought is *only* a thought. When you don't like the one you have, choose another.

Just remember, in order for a new thought to have any real power, it has to be an authentic expression of oneself. (Anthony, Lester, and Lisa were not certain how things would unfold, but they were authentically and intentionally engaged in accomplishing their goals.)

ABOUT YOUR IDENTIFY

In order to attain a sense of freedom in your life, you have to be willing to transcend your identity. By *transcend*, I mean to go beyond. By identity, I mean *identifying yourself as the sum of your collective parts*—that is, your name, age, height, career, relationships, religion, wealth, education, IQ, beliefs, likes, and dislikes.

Most of us are pretty attached to our identity, our sense of who we are. What if you reframed how you view yourself so that you related to all those qualities and characteristics as just that? They are just labels, words that describe various traits and characteristics.

That's not who you are! So, you ask, if I'm not my identity, *who am I?*

Great question. There are literally thousands of books on the subject. Some are very deep, like Ken Wilbur's *Transformations of Consciousness.* Some more spiritual, like Michael Singer's *The Untethered Soul, the Journey Beyond Yourself* or Eckhart Tolle's *A New Earth: Awakening to Your Life's Purpose.*[5]

For our purpose, who you are, in fact, who we all are, is the possibility of the unbound, unlimited expression of being human.

Each of us manifests this possibility in a totally unique fashion based on our individual and distinct set of internal conversations. Although there are billions of people on the planet, no one has had the same history or experiences as you have. No one has had the same successes or failures. No one has made the same decisions and choices that you have. Therefore, no one is having the same internal conversations that you are having.

This brings us to a tipping point: if you can get that you *have* thoughts and feelings but are not your thoughts and feelings, that you *have* an identity but are not your identity, then you may be ready to take a bold step forward in achieving freedom.

Consider the possibility that *your word is who you are.*

Try on, *I am my word.*
- Who you are is your words, both external and internal.
- There are no throwaway conversations. They all count.
- Every conversation you have with others has an impact on them.

---

5   Tolle, *A New Earth.*

- Every conversation you have with yourself has an impact on you.
- When you say you are committed to something or someone, you are committing yourself.
- When you give someone your word, you are giving them YOU.

Until you take ownership of your word, the conversations that are occurring own you. And so long as the conversations own you, you can't exercise the power of choice that will liberate you into a transformed future.

This may sound strange or difficult to grasp at first, but consider the power you can gain if the one person in the world who has always had the say, and always will get to say how things are, is you.

A bit overwhelming? Just remember the answer to the question, how do you walk a mile? The answer is one step at a time.

Certainly, coming to terms with yourself, owning your life, and being responsible for your experience is a huge request. But, what's the alternative? Once you get it, once you recognize the accuracy of the conversation, it doesn't make sense to bury your head in the sand or ignore that you are indeed responsible for yourself.

10

THE POWER OF CHOICE

The Transitions Process does not offer a cure. I'm not in that business. The Transitions Process offers you a choice: the opportunity to choose between can't and can, won't and will, going it alone or creating partnerships, resignation or commitment, and ultimately, the most important choice of all, reacting to past successes and failures or creating a future of your own choosing.

ACT 2

"There are no second acts in life," F. Scott Fitzgerald wrote in his notebook while working on his final novel, *The Last Tycoon*. The quote is quite famous, good for more than fifty thousand hits on Google. However, it is also famously and incredibly wrong! American life is full of second acts. The only impediment to getting there is what's going on inside us, the internal conversations that do so much to shape who we have been, where we are today, and what we are headed toward. And here's the really good news:

It's only a conversation. You can choose to change it.

Leave that voice on automatic pilot, fail to actively manage it on behalf of your chosen future, and it will deliver one basic message time and time again, month after month, year after year: "We got through the first ten thousand days of your life, and we will get through the next ten thousand." All of which is fine, if the status quo is your goal and just surviving is at the top of your bucket list.

For many of us, our internal conversations cast a shadow on our days, even before we get out of the shower. Everyone recognizes these conversations: *I can't make the deadline. I won't get the promotion. I don't make enough to make ends meet. Why explain myself? No one will believe me anyway. It's too late.* By the time you towel off, it *is* too late. We find ourselves dragged back into the familiar swamp of disappointments and challenges, and survival seems like the best possible outcome.

Like it or not, we can't turn the conversations off. But we can choose to create new alternative conversations to replace the old ones. In other words, you can choose *not* to listen to old, limited ones. You can choose *I CAN* instead of *I can't*, *I WILL* instead of *I won't*, and *I DO* instead of *I don't*.

Words, of course, are only words, but as an expression of choice, an expression of our true intentions and commitments, they have power.

Here are some examples of clients who made a choice to go beyond their predictable futures and create a future of their own choosing.

CAROLYN'S CHALLENGE

Carolyn was one of only a handful of senior vice presidents at a global leader in banking, a job that brought tremendous daily pressures and required her to work an average of twelve hours a day, six days a week. Carolyn was a mother of two teenagers (a daughter in high school and a son heading there soon), and she didn't want to miss this last, critical part of their childhoods, as she had missed so many earlier moments.

Carolyn had convinced herself that the corporate culture of the bank didn't care about her dilemma, and further, that no one in her industry and position could successfully balance family and work without sacrificing one or the other on the altar of expediency. So she resigned herself to seeking a tolerable level of unhappiness. She couldn't bring herself to quit after putting in so much time chasing the brass ring, and she could not ignore the maternal conversation that raged in her head. But she would survive, get from moment to moment, from day to day, and deal with the imbalance as well as she could.

SHIFTING THE CONVERSATION

Given the opportunity to stop, look, and identify the conversations that were driving her actions and feelings, Carolyn recognized that her core commitment, the one she had to respond to, was to be with her kids more, to be available to them in their teens.

She created a new conversation, which at first seemed unrealistic. "I *can* be there for my kids and still do my job." By shifting the conversations from one in which being a mother and doing the job were at odds, to one in which she *was* going to be a great mother and still do her job, in that order, she found the power to tell her superiors that this was the way it had to be. To her surprise, her boss was more than willing to accede to Carolyn's request that she arrange her schedule to be home more often and at better hours to support her family.

ED'S STORY

Ed was trapped by his own success. A dentist, he had put together a highly profitable chain of suburban orthodontic clinics, ringing across a major West Coast city. He had built his practice to make money, and he was making it hand over fist. But Ed had also structured the company so he could have total control over every facet of it, and he no longer did. The dentists and health professionals who worked for him complained constantly about schedules, bonuses, unordered equipment, and long-festering personnel issues.

Ed told his employees they were out of touch with the real world. At a deeper level, he knew that he was, in fact, responsible for the success of the practice and that the practice was giving way at the seams. To make matters worse, Ed's reputation had become that he was an unapproachable horse's ass.

Ed's aggressiveness, arrogance, dismissive attitude, short fuse, and many other unlovable qualities seemed built into his DNA. In fact, these qualities were the result of choices Ed had been making for decades to advance his own agenda. Tell Ed that a hygienist in the Westside office was falling short of the mark, and he reacted as though it were a personal, full-scale attack on his leadership.

To make matters worse, Ed had never really shared authority for the business, and at this point, he could no longer effectively manage the multi-facility practice he had created.

As part of the Transitions Process, I ask clients to reach out to peers, family, and friends to get a ground-level accounting of the benefits and costs associated with their behavior. Ed did that, and in the wake of what he learned, he realized that dominating and controlling those around him had a huge cost.

SHIFTING THE CONVERSATION

Ed saw that he did indeed have a choice. He could continue with the status quo ("This is the way I am; too bad. Deal with it or leave."), which clearly wasn't working, or he could choose to accept his flaws and create a new set of internal conversations that acknowledged those flaws but gave birth to a real commitment to move beyond them. That's exactly what he did.

He declared his intention to completely reinvent himself. At first, there were many who doubted his expressions of regret, his asking for forgiveness, and his commitment to change. Initially, they resisted his offers to delegate authority and responsibility. But over time, the staff recognized Ed's behavior and attitudes had shifted. It wasn't a 180-degree shift, and he did slip back more than he would have liked, but with time, the cumulative effect of his choice to share power and interact with others collegially had an enormous influence on everyone concerned.

MIKE'S STORY

In my first meeting with Mike, he said something that was startling. He said, "I own many companies. I have thousands of employees. I don't have any friends. I just want to have friends." Mike, in fact, had many issues to deal with, but at the heart of them all was his absolute preoccupation with his own self-importance. Mike was convinced that everyone around him was thrilled to play a supporting part to his starring role. This, I pointed out, was not a formula for friendship or even much of a life.

Mike was more than a therapist's meal ticket. He was the kind of client who sends a shrink's kids through college and grad school. But helping Mike understand his raging narcissism—*I'm number one and everyone's thrilled with it!*—was never going to get him the friend-filled future he ardently desired.

Number ones, it turns out, are often attracted to other number ones. They share common experiences, have common problems, and talk the same language, even when they are pursuing very different endeavors. (Think not only Gates and Buffet, but also Bono and Henry Kissinger.) Mike was never going to stop thinking of himself as top dog, but by shifting his internal conversation from *I* to *we,* Mike projected himself into a future in which he mentored others similarly inclined to achieve number-one status in their individual fields. Those newly minted fellow top dogs became his ever-growing network of friends.

SHIFTING THE CONVERSATION

A simple choice to shift his perspective from competing to contributing made all the difference. As for my specific part in all this, it was minimal, at least on the surface. I couldn't lay hands on Mike and command him to be someone he's not. I'm not that good. But I *could* point out to him that he did have a choice to continue with his friendless past or to commit to a friend-enriched future and begin building the infrastructure that would make it happen. And I *could* ask him to listen carefully to the conversation he was having around that choice.

The Transitions Process is about having a choice and choosing on behalf of your own future, choosing where you want to go in life. Make that choice in the present, while targeting the future. Align your actions now with intentional results to come, and you have a purposeful combination that in the end will free you from whatever in the past has been holding you back.

VANESSA'S STORY

Vanessa had a very different problem. She had been married for twenty years, was the mother of two middle-schoolers, and was enjoying the luxury of watching them grow up at close quarters, thanks to her husband's highly successful law practice. Vanessa was now trying to prepare for act two, which included what became for her the central part of her existence. Vanessa was gay and had taken a secret lover eighteen months earlier. Her husband, she thought, would probably be civil about a breakup. They had grown increasingly distant during the last decade or more. But that wasn't what brought Vanessa to my door. Did she have to continue hiding her sexuality if she wanted to keep her children in her life or could she design a life that included both?

I told her I couldn't make that choice for her or even begin to predict the outcome. All I knew for certain was that if she were authentically committed to keeping her children firmly in a life that included her true sexual orientation and her lover, then she would be giving them two choices in return. The choice was a specific one *(take your mother as she is or risk losing her)* or a more general one *(live in a past in which this hasn't happened, or organize a future around the fact it has)*.

I've amassed plenty of evidence kids can deal surprisingly well with choices like that. But did Vanessa trust her relationship with her children enough to believe they would say yes to a future that included a gay mother deeply involved in their lives? That was the bigger question. When Vanessa said yes to that, it was only a matter of *how* to tell the children, not *if* to tell them. That was a much easier conversation.

PAUL'S STORY

This is a true success tale and an example of how little effort it often takes to move away mountains of frustration. I got a call one day from Paul, a client I had previously worked with. The problem now was his teenage son, Brian.

"He's worthless," Paul said. "He's no good. He's ruining his life, and mine, with this crazy band shit!"

"You're saying he's a bad person?"

"Oh, no," he answered. "The kid is just sort of confused, lacking any real direction."

I suggested Paul reinterpret who his son was. Instead of relating to Brian as if he's "no good," what if Paul chose to say, "My son is a brilliant, artistic person who hasn't quite found his self-expression yet"?

That changed everything, because everything that had been troubling Paul about his son's past and present could now fit inside a new understanding of, and commitment to, the future Brian was headed toward. The next time Paul looked at his son, he wasn't seeing a wasteful kid avoiding responsibility (which sounds, of course, very much like a teenage boy) but as this amazing possibility who hadn't yet landed on a positive expression. Again, a small change—and a very large transformation.

As it turned out, Brian shifted from music to painting and drawing, which, to everyone's surprise, he was quite good at. Brian chose to go back to school and get a degree in architecture and is now one of the more creative real estate designers in Dallas.

CORPORATIONS ARE NETWORKS OF CONVERSATIONS

As with my clients, so with the companies I've worked with. The stage is bigger and the clients more diffuse, but the ultimate issues are the same. Do they want to live in the past or the future? Are they going to be *I or we* organizations? Do they want to be organized around simply returning a profit to investors, or are they willing to also be a place where people are inspired to contribute their talents and gifts to the corporate cause? Put in its simplest terms, are they more interested in preserving the status quo or in committing themselves, management, *and* frontline workers to a future that is not a group life sentence?

THE OIL PATCH

Two decades ago, one of the major oil companies working in the Gulf of Mexico requested help to solve what seemed at first an actuarial dilemma. Oil was selling at between $10 and $20 a barrel, well below total extraction costs in the Gulf's deep water. Could we suggest some way around the balance sheet? In fact, we could.

Execs, roughhouse drillers, and all stations in between were stuck in survival mode. The turning point came when management chose to fully involve all their employees in creating a solution. They chose to empower and listen to their employees as a resource rather than as a complaint or one more budget item on the balance sheet. By freeing them to commit to a future in which the numbers balanced in their favor, we obligated all parties to create an infrastructure that could make that happen. Suddenly, previously silent workers on the front line were coming up with new ways to drill more accurately in half the time. It didn't matter if the price of oil went up, although it did; extraction costs tumbled.

ONE OF THE LARGEST FURNITURE PRODUCERS

Much more recently, we were called in by a large furniture manufacturer to deal with a factory in which almost a third of all materials were being rejected by purchasers at the wholesale or retail levels. Management was considering closing the facility, and indeed, we were the workers' last hope. By empowering the front line to find its own solutions and committing workers, individually and collectively, to zero defects, we not only helped turn the situation around; we also sowed the seeds for what has become one of the most efficient facilities in the entire corporate empire.

11
SELF-GENERATION

Reinventing your life is no longer an option. It is an imperative!

In truth, we are constantly reinventing our lives. But as we have shown in previous chapters, most often we *double down* on the same formulas for getting by, for just getting through life.

It's like a *Peanuts* cartoon I recently saw. One day Snoopy visits a pet store. He's deeply distressed, because he sees all his animal kingdom compatriots locked in cages like prisoners. But then a wonderful idea comes to him. Looking around, he notices the coast is clear, and he runs down the aisle opening all the doors, crying, "You're free! You're free! You're free!"

But when he looks back, he sees that all the animals are still huddled in their cages, cowering as far as possible from the open doors, overwhelmed by the new opportunities that have suddenly been made available. Snoopy runs back down the aisle, closing all the cage doors, yelling, "You're safe! You're safe! You're safe!"

When it comes to your life, the answers are not that simple. Snoopy is not going to come running down the aisle to close your cage doors. No one gets to hang out in a warm, comfortable space anymore. *Welcome to the twenty-first century!*

Change, no matter what form it takes, has the power to suddenly and unexpectedly disrupt and threaten what we have planned for the future. Job and career security is fiction. The traditional family structure is a statistical oddity. Financial stability has been replaced by wild swings in one's net worth or asset base. And good health, which once seemed a given, becomes more uncertain by the year.

Nothing buys us a way out of this new world. And yet, it is possible to shape what happens to us. These transition points or events can also be incredibly valuable. They can reveal radically different opportunities to create a future.

The key to successfully redesigning the future starts with understanding how to take advantage of these openings. In the following pages, I will explicitly reveal the true nature of change. With this knowledge in hand, you will be free to act in tune with your core values, desires, and hopes for the future.

DISTINGUISHING PAST, PRESENT, AND FUTURE

Have you ever been in the past? Have you ever lived in the future? The answer is always no. In the way we view life, we have created an artificial reality based on past, present, and future. But the fact is that human beings have never lived anyplace other than the present.

Still, the concept of past, present, and future is a maze many people spend their lives trapped inside. Because they don't understand they've never been anywhere else but the present, people constantly ruminate about the past, as if by going over it again and again, something will change. (Why did I invest in that business? Why did I marry him?) They spend an enormous amount of their psychic energy attempting to reshuffle facts from the past to create a more desirable future for themselves. But it doesn't work!

One woman keeps telling her current husband about how

her former husband cheated on her. She has trouble trusting her new husband in their current relationship. Unfortunately, the new husband finds himself living in a condition of not being trusted, being under suspicion, and being checked up on, all based on absolutely nothing from their current marriage.

THE PAST

The past is, of course, the realm in which we reflect on what we already know—our assessments, judgments, understandings, histories, justifications, explanations, rationales, and reasons. Just to be clear, imagine you are at a tennis match. You're sitting in the stands with a friend, watching two players go at it with each other. Just for fun, let's say it's Serena Williams and Maria Sharapova, both world-class professionals.

If you stop to notice, you can see that after each point you have a reaction—happiness, disappointment, excitement, or frustration—all a function of which player you are rooting for and who won the point. The operative words in the previous sentence are *after* (each point) and *reaction*. In fact, you are reacting to something that has already occurred—something in the past.

How odd that we spend the majority of our time having conversations about what has already happened. Regardless of our interpretations, opinions, or feelings, the point is over and the score won't change.

THE PRESENT

The present can be defined as what's happening right now . . . now, now, now. And if you examine what is happening for human beings in the present, we are acting, thinking, and feeling. That is what's occurring! And as long as we are having past-based conversations (with ourselves or others), those assessments, judgments, et cetera have a profound and determining effect on what gets acted upon and experienced in the present. Thus, most likely, more of the same.

Can you change the past? No—it's over. Can you change the present? No—it's too late. You're already doing it. If you want to change your life, you must go to the future. You have to get out in front of where you are now to alter the direction your life is headed.

THE FUTURE

Only the future is undetermined and open. The fundamental truth about the future is that something either *will* or *won't* happen—period. You go to get into your car. It will or won't be there. It will or won't start. You fall in love and get married. You either will or won't stay married. It is the domain where possibilities, commitments, and intentions can be brought into existence, leading to actions.

LEARNING HOW TO LIVE FROM THE FUTURE, INSTEAD OF LIVING FROM THE PAST

Living life from the past, from your experience and past learning, produces a default future that can only be an expression of the past. If you want to create a life that's not an extension of who you've already been, you must live your life from the future. How? By generating and acting on inner dialogues that are based on your intentions and commitments for the future.

You can choose which conversations get mental airtime and expression in your life. But first, you must be able to identify the primary types of inner conversations:

- Conversations for the Future: Based in possibility and
                                   commitment.

- Conversations for the Present: Produce action and experience (thinking and feeling).
- Conversations from the Past: Consist of stories, reasons, histories, and explanations.

To begin creating your designed future—the future that you'd love to have—try the following:

- First, write down what it would look like—for example, "I will be a successful playwright!" in the future column.
- Now, in the past column, write down the answers to the question why you haven't achieved that desired future. *(No time. Can't afford it. May not be talented enough.)*

Here's an example:

FUTURE	PRESENT	PAST
Commitments & Possibilities	Actions & Experience	History, reasons, explanations
1. Great playwright		1. No time
2. Awards		2. No money
3. Broadway play		3. No talent

Now, you try it:

First, write down your desired future. Next, write down the reasons and explanations why you have not reached that future.

Invariably, the column representing the past becomes filled with stories, excuses, and reasons. The action that one takes in the present is either going to be an expression of the past or the desired future.

The only place where anything ever is expressed is in the present. Both the past-based interpretations and future commitments fight for airtime in the present. Past-based inner dialogues are automatic. They're already there. So, if you want your future commitments and possibilities to get airtime, to be expressed, to start to be available to build upon, you've got to consciously build a set of practices that allow for the manifestation of the future.

In other words, it's not sufficient to *have* commitments. You need to develop practices for *being committed* to your commitments. Everyone wants to be healthy and in good shape, but that commitment, if not acted on, does us little good. We need to have practices, such as going to the gym three days a week or maintaining a certain diet that leads to good health.

12
SPEECH ACT THEORY

Speech Act Theory is the study of how words can be used as actions. The originator of this theory was John Austin, whose paper, "How to Do Things with Words," divided language into three different categories, including a category called performatives. According to Austin, performatives allow individuals to perform an act through speaking.

A request is one form of performative. When you say the word *pen*, a pen doesn't literally fall from your mouth. But when you say, "I request that you pick up the pen," a request does literally fall from your mouth. In the moment of uttering the words, an action happens. A request occurs.

DECLARATIONS

In the beginning, there is the word—your word.

> Words move the world. Human beings have the capacity to invent themselves day by day, moment by moment, through their words.

For example, when two people get in front of a priest, rabbi, or justice of the peace and take their marriage vows, they are inventing a shared future. When the couple responds "I do" to the question "Do you take this person?" they have created a whole new world to live into. They go forward as a "we," taking responsibility for each other's lives and happiness. The official then declares, "I now pronounce you married." The act of declaring changes not only *us* but also the world we live in.

The German philosopher Martin Heidegger referred to language as the house of being for human beings. Declare your future in uncertain terms, and the future will be uncertain. Declare your future with power, purpose, and conviction, and your declarations will have a life force.

Leaders the world over have relied on the power of declaring:

Gandhi: "We will stand in front of the salt gates and let them strike us. We will not depart, and they will leave our country."

Martin Luther King, quoting Langston Hughes: "America never was America to me. And yet I swear this oath—America will be."

The Declaration of Independence: "We hold these truths to be self-evident, that all men are created equal, that they are endowed by their Creator with certain unalienable Rights, that among these are Life, Liberty and the Pursuit of Happiness."

John F. Kennedy: "I believe that this nation should commit itself to achieving the goal, before the decade is out, of landing a man on the moon and returning him safely to Earth."

Declarations aren't facts when first spoken. They originate as a possibility to be *lived into.* The act of causing a future to become a *reality* originates as a declaration. Through the declaration, we say who we are and, equally important, what we stand for.

It's okay to have some fun when creating declarations. Play with them. Swing out. Give yourself permission to step out.

To use the example of a writer working on a play, instead of merely declaring, "I am going to write a play," step out and try, "I am a playwright of immense commitment and talent, contributing a work that will transport audiences into an incredible and unforgettable new world."

> To be really powerful, you must be willing to risk the present as you know it for an unpredictable future.
>
> —Fernando Flores

DECLARATIONS: THE POWER TO BE

The basic form of declaration is "X is so because I say so."

A few examples: "I'm going to marry that girl." Why? "Because I say so." No justifications are required. An umpire declares, "Strike one!" It is a strike because he said so. No proof or evidence is required. As a matter of fact, you and I are declaring what's so (and ourselves) into existence moment by moment by moment. Perhaps the two most powerful words in the English language are "I am."

"I am" is a powerful, life-generating declaration. Declarations sound familiar and we make them so often that they go unnoticed.

I am hot.

I am hungry.

I am tired.

I am happy.

I am committed.

Can you see that whatever you say *you are*, for you, that's the truth? You are! Other forms of the same principle are:

I am able to pick you up at 3:00 p.m.

I will call you tonight.

I can meet you at 6:00 p.m. for dinner.

I am going to complete the marathon.

This last sentence has magical properties. In the present (I am) declaring a future to be fulfilled. In the present, I am already that future (completing the race).

I will go to medical school. I am (in the present) going to go (in the future) to medical school.

I am going to take that job. Or, *I will* take that job.

These are all forms of declarations, and to the extent that you are making declarations as an authentic expression of your intentions and commitments for the future, these declarations have power.

Before we discuss what futures you might be willing to commit to, let's take a look at what you are already committed to. Remember, you can't commit to going left and right at the same time. So whatever you are already committed to, or committing to, *now, now, now* gets top billing and the highest probability of shaping our actions and experience.

For example, if I'm committed to my relationship, to being monogamous, and someone starts flirting with me, I may appreciate it, but I will probably also discourage the conversation from proceeding down a slippery slope. If I am not truly committed to my partner, I may encourage the flirtatious conversation and wind up in a situation that I will find difficult to explain tomorrow.

CREATING YOUR FUTURE

What would you be doing, whom would you be with, and what

kind of relationships would you have if you had the freedom to say? I say, *I declare,* that you do have the freedom to say. You can literally declare your future in every area of your life—relationships, career, family, mental and physical health, finances, philanthropy, education, spirituality, leisurely pursuits, and so on.

I encourage you to be extraordinarily generous with yourself in declaring your future. You can always modify and pare back later, but for now, step out as far as you can possibly imagine. Make your declarations an expression of what is in your heart and soul. Remember, the only way of gaining access to your dreams is to first put them into language and then act on them.

AUTHENTIC DECLARATIONS OF SELF VERSUS FANTASY

It's important to recognize the difference between an authentic declaration and a fantasy. If your declaration is founded only on your desires, wants, or needs but lacks commitment, it won't have the power to get over the bridge of time and into reality. For example, you can declare that you're going to be the CEO of a major corporation. But if you don't really think you could be, then you won't take the appropriate actions. You won't put yourself into the necessary school of hard knocks that produces CEOs.

Yes, declarations are risky. They come with no guarantees. But to shy away from declaring, to not access your God-given power to create your life, is like buying a car without a gas pedal.

LIVING THE FUTURE NOW

How do you bridge the gap between declarations and reality?

Through action.

REQUESTS AND PROMISES

Just as it takes action to transform a blueprint into a building, it requires being in action to turn your vision/declarations into results.

Human beings are capable of creating extraordinary visions in their minds. ("I'm going to be the world's greatest skater!") But the litmus test is: Does the person then take the appropriate actions to fulfill the commitment? Do they hire a coach, buy the equipment, and spend countless hours in training? If they do *not*, their dreams of greatness remain just that, dreams. If they *do* take action, they invariably begin by having many conversations with others to advance themselves. Besides expressing their dreams, they undoubtedly engage in discussions, in which they express and elicit from others a series of commitments involving promises and requests.

"I request that you be my coach and train me for the next twelve months."

"I promise to pay you one hundred dollars an hour to coach me."

The more audacious the goal, the bolder the promises and requests.

REQUESTS

Requests are defined as: *I request that you do X by Y, where X is some action and Y is some time.* As in, "Mary, I request that we get together today and call Allen at 5:30 p.m. to discuss the merger." Notice the all-important time element. Requests without time are not requests, because there's no commitment involved. Consider the following: "Let's get together later." "Of course, I'll pay you back." "Let's have lunch." Until these have a specific time, they lack commitment.

COMMITTED RESPONSES TO REQUESTS

Let's look at four possible committed responses to a request. Here's the request: I request that you deposit Tom's check in his account by 3:00 p.m. today.

Response 1: Yes, *(I promise)* to deposit Tom's check in his account by 3:00 p.m. today.

Response 2: No, *(I decline)* to deposit Tom's check in his account by 3:00 p.m. today.

Response 3: No, and *(counteroffer)* I offer to deposit the check in Tom's account before 10:00 a.m. tomorrow.

Response 4: I will let you know by noon today *(commit to commit)* if I will commit to depositing Tom's check in his account by 3:00 p.m. today.

Responses such as, *I will try, I think I can, why not, and I'll get back to you* all lack commitment and are, therefore, not acceptable. It is very common for people to ask others to do something without specifying a time frame. This is the easy way out for both the requestor and the requestee. After all, how do you hold someone accountable if the conversation goes something like, "You said you would pay me back the fifty dollars I lent you. Where is it?" And the response is, "Don't worry. I told you I'd pay you back." Yuck! Who would want to live in that quagmire? Yet many of us do.

PROMISES

Promises are defined as: *I promise to do X by Y.* Like requests, promises require a specific time. Promises are most powerful when made to someone else, not just you. There are people who will allow you to get away with things. Others won't. If someone is truly committed to fulfilling a goal, they are likely to choose partners who will hold them to their word.

LIVING THE FUTURE NOW

Consider for a moment a really unusual notion. When you speak, you're not merely offering the world *words*. You're offering yourself. The listener is getting you, not just your words. When you listen, you are not just hearing what someone is saying. You're interpreting what is said and, thus, creating *your* reality. (You might hear a song you think is moving, while another thinks it's ordinary.) The act of listening is not passive. In fact, the world *occurs* for each individual as a match for our personal interpretations.

When you speak, you're not merely uttering words. You are creating your reality. You're generating an expression of yourself. This applies when speaking to others and when speaking to yourself as well. When you commit to yourself, saying, "Today, I'm writing my play," you are giving your word. By honoring your conversations, by honoring your word, you empower yourself.

Of course, not every day will be perfect. When lapses in living from your commitments occur, be generous to yourself. Acknowledge that you're in training. You're a human being. Recognize that lapses will happen. That doesn't reduce the commitment that you have made to yourself.

When you find yourself in a negative, past-based conversation, stop. Recognize the conversation for what it is. Do not empower "I can't" or "I'm not able" conversations.

Start by describing what the desired future looks like. When you are the best skater in the world, what will become available? Olympic medals? Recognition? Appreciation? Relationships? Endorsements? Embellish the vision as much as possible. The more time you allow yourself to dwell in the experience and imagine what it will be like, the clearer the blueprint will be in your mind. This supports you to go and get the right people, materials, and resources to begin building.

13
CHANGE IS A SUPERSTITION

Before we move to *how* to build your future, I want to go back to a promise I made, to reveal the true nature of change. Consider the following: change is a superstition.

As I previously stated, you can't change the past. It's already over. If I spilled a cup of coffee in my lap, I can't go back in time and change whether that happened or not.

You can't change the present if our definition of the present is what's happening now, now, now, because once again, too late. If the coffee is currently being spilled, I can't *unspill it.*

And here's the kicker. You can't change the future, because it hasn't happened yet. You can't change something that isn't.

So, if you can't change the past, present, or future, I assert that you can't change anything. Well, if I'm not changing things, if I'm not changing my opinion or the way I choose to go home to avoid the traffic up ahead, what am I doing? Great question!

Consider that rather than changing what you are experiencing or doing, you are creating your experience, your next action, moment by moment. We are creating next, next, next. That's the gift God has given us. We have the opportunity to create our lives now, now, now. Perhaps we really are created in God's (the Creator's) image.

The shift from *change* to *create* alters your life. You are now living into your future. You are actually living from the future you are about to create. This is really powerful. All that's required is your willingness to be the author, the creator of your experience, your life. You have the opportunity and privilege of being the creator of your*self*.

Notice I didn't say you create the circumstances with which you have to engage. I didn't say you create the rainstorm. I am saying you are responsible for creating your relationships with the rainstorm. You either accept it or resent it. You either move forward with your plans or you create a new plan. Whatever you choose, you are creating your experience. You are creating your relationship and reaction to all that is occurring.

And where does this choosing occur? In your internal conversation, that's where. How does all this creating occur? By virtue of your conversations.

If in fact we are creating our lives, then I suggest that we shift our focus from "How can I change me?" to "How can I create? How do I create?"

This can be *relanguaged*, reworded, into very simple but powerful questions: How can I master the game of creating? Can I get at the source of the nature of this phenomenon of creating one's life?

To paraphrase Heidegger, "Language is the home of being within which man dwells."

So, this once again brings us back full circle to our internal conversation. The degree to which we have something to say (to ourselves) about what the internal conversations are saying, we have freedom and power. *Power* has to do with our ability to cause outcomes, to bring our intentions into reality. *Freedom* has to do with choice.

Here is a very incomplete set of rules and guidelines I offer my clients for creating conversations.

RULES FOR CREATING AND CHOOSING CONVERSATIONS

1) Don't intentionally hurt yourself, or anyone else, for that matter.

2) Forgive yourself and others. Forgiveness is a magic tonic.

3) Don't promote your limitations. If you say you *can't*, then you can't.

4) Start wherever you are and go forward. It's the only way you can go.

5) As you are going forward, any issue that needs to get addressed will present itself. These are the ones to address, not everything from the past.

6) Compassion is a useful tool for human beings. None of us was given a manual on how to live life successfully. Most of us wake up every day with an intention to do the best we can, to do better. Life is, in fact, challenging to say the least.

7) Don't resist your thoughts. That causes their persistence.

8) Talk about your concerns to someone you trust. If you don't trust anyone, tell a tree or write yourself a letter. In your head, negative thoughts fester. Say them aloud and the likelihood

of a more favorable outcome improves. Don't try to *sell* your thoughts. Don't try to convince others. Just say them. Then be open for support and feedback.

9) Meditate. This is a way to focus, relax, relieve stress, and get yourself clear. A little self-time goes a long way.

10) Others want to help, but remember that not everyone is able to. You are the judge of what is helpful or not.

11) If you are in a bad situation, don't wait for someone to get you out of it. Take action. Asking for help is an action.

12) Once again, much if not all your experience (including your feelings) is directly matched to your internal conversation. Can you hear what you are telling yourself? That's your world! If you are telling yourself you are bored, you are. If you are telling yourself you are tired, you are. If your mind is saying that you don't want to see someone, you don't!

This is a very important insight to understand. *Your reality is a perfect match for your internal conversation. That's right. Your moods, attitudes, feelings, and emotions are all tied to your individual internal conversation.*

WE CAN

TRANSFORMATION MADE EASY

14

SELF-ACTUALIZATION

The fourth and final phase of the Transitions Process is called self-actualization. This is a term that was introduced by Kurt Goldstein in 1934. He presented self-actualization as "the tendency to actualize, as much as possible, the individual's capacities in the world."

Under Goldstein's influence, Abraham Maslow developed a hierarchical theory of human motivation in *Motivation and Personality* in 1954.

Maslow's book started a psychological revolution out of which grew humanistic psychology. Maslow defines self-actualization as "the desire for self-fulfillment, the desire to become more and more of what one is, to become everything that one is capable of becoming." Many textbooks define self-actualization simply as "the full realization of one's potential and one's true self."

So what is one's true self?

I believe that a true self is a transformed self. Transformed individuals are knowing participants in the conscious evolution of humanity and the evolution of human consciousness.

They embrace the notion that conditions such as poverty or

99

hunger do not exist in isolation but rather in relation to a larger context of living systems. Transformative individuals are conscious of the interconnected nature of all life and set about doing the work of raising the tide, not just their boats.

Werner Erhard produced an event in the late 1970s called "A World That Works for Everyone, with No One and Nothing Left Out." This program captured the spirit of this orientation to being alive and having a life that makes a difference.

Interestingly, I think it follows that true happiness is experienced when an individual experiences being connected to another or others while living intentionally in the space of contribution.

We are all on a journey, living our adventurous lives on planet Earth together. Anything of substance that we accomplish will involve and affect others. Therefore, one of the most important sets of conversations that we need to be conscious of, and not leave to chance or historical tendencies, is our set of conversations *for being related*. For being more related. For being better related. For being as generous as possible to others.

What if we actually create each other through our conversations and acts of listening? The most generous gift we can give ourselves, therefore, is to be generous to others. But generosity goes even further than that. By living and acting generously, we create a world in which it is easier to *be*.

By understanding that our way of being with others affects reality and what's possible, we change our orientation from reliving the past to opening the door to the future. Generosity also alters our relationships by opening us up to the creative contributions of others.

While independence represented the gold ring in the old world of survival ("Look at me! Look at what I've achieved!"), interdependence and collaboration are expressions of our twenty-first-century community for those of us who are lucky enough to have gained access to our core aspirations. The resources, support, and contributions of others are key to creating the future we want.

By shifting our conversations from focusing on ourselves to making a difference and contributing to others, surprisingly, we experience a sense of freedom. We begin to feel a natural connection and compassion for the world and those in it. It's a shift in perspective from taking and owning to giving and sharing—a generosity that links us to the planet. We care about healing that which needs healing. We see the possibility of providing service in the places where our gifts would be of benefit. It's not an urge that arises out of guilt or obligation but because we feel so deeply connected to the beauty and vulnerability of the planet and those who share it with us. We just want to help.

Recently, I participated in a journey into the Ecuadorian rain forest. Our group of thirty Westerners, led by Bill and Lynne Twist, founders of the Pachamama Alliance, were there to partner with the Achuar indigenous natives to preserve their homelands and avoid being displaced by big oil.

Dr. Choe, an extraordinary accupressurist, joined us on the trip. The natives would have no part of his healing skills. Then the chief of the tribe told Dr. Choe through an interpreter that his wife had severe back pains and could not walk or move normally. The chief asked if Dr. Choe could help.

For the next ten to fifteen minutes, Dr. Choe pressed, twisted, and manipulated her body in a way that was frightening to watch. Then he asked her to get up and walk. To everyone's amazement, she walked upright, gracefully and without pain. For the next several days, there was a line outside Dr. Choe's cabin, each person waiting to receive a "miracle" treatment.

> We each have a gift to bring into the world. In order to make a difference, you do not need to be perfect or even the best in your trade.

POSSIBILITY

For example, Deb, a very successful producer, wanted to write a script of her own. After several attempts that always resulted in incomplete and less-than-inspired material, she gave up trying. During her Transitions Process, this repeated failure showed up as one of the major incompletions in her life. When asked why she thought that despite her commitment and perceived talent she was unable to produce a script, her immediate response was, "I never had the time to focus on it and get it right."

Even when she tried to make the time, something always came up and distracted Deb from her mission. Sounds reasonable and perhaps familiar, doesn't it? *She didn't have the time to focus and get it right.*

Then something *magical* happened. Just by saying aloud what she had been saying to herself for years, she heard something else. Her whole body started shaking. She yelled, "Oh my God! I have misunderstood the 'stop' this whole time. I've blamed the lack of focused time on my inability to create the script. But now I see clearly I've been stopped by my concern to get it right."

There's no freedom, no self-expression, in trying to get it right. During the next three months, Deb found her voice and generated a script that she was truly excited about. It hasn't been sold to a network yet, but for her that was not the point. She said, "I was amazed to see how completely I shut down my own creativity when I could have been generating a different reality all along. It's a huge awakening."

Far from perfect, Kevin, an entrepreneur running his own company, related a personal story. "I've always focused entirely on my work. I've given lip service to my commitment to my family. My nine-year-old son frequently asked me to practice soccer with him, and I always came up with some excuse. 'I'm too tired. I'm too busy.' Somehow, it didn't register with me how costly not being available actually was."

Kevin continued, saying, "During my Transitions Process, I learned to listen differently. I stopped pushing my own agenda and started listening to my son. In spite of being terrible at all sports, including soccer, I started to make time for him. We got out there and practiced several times a week. I told him I was sorry for not being a better coach, and he said, 'I don't care. I just love us playing together.' I couldn't hold back the tears. What was I waiting for? Fortunately, I not only had a breakthrough with my son but also learned that by being attentive and interested in others, I became more interesting *and* happy!"

Once again, no need to be perfect. What made the difference was Kevin's commitment to his relationship with his son.

A FINAL STORY

Philip was the chairman of the board of a Fortune 100 company. He was accustomed to people saying yes and doing his bidding. He did not relish a challenge to his view or authority.

Unfortunately for Philip, his wife of thirty years was not about to play a subordinate role. She stood her ground and expressed herself fully at all times (probably the reason the relationship lasted thirty years). Philip, to his credit, recognized he had to alter the way he communicated and reacted to his wife, but he had no idea how to begin.

With a little coaching, he was able to start to hear his own conversations. They were very directive and demanding. There was not much in the way of collaboration or partnership. Philip saw the enormous cost in terms of happiness, satisfaction, affinity, and love between him and his wife. He now saw he was responsible for what he had previously blamed others for.

What he then said was quite surprising. "Believe it or not, I find it to be a great relief that a lot of the problems my wife and I were having were caused by me. That's because if I am the problem, I can do something about it, right now!"

It all starts with being related. The quality of our relationships exists as a function of our conversations, both our speaking and our listening. At the core of our *being*, at the foundation of our *existence*, is how we relate to ourselves and how we relate to others. Most important is how *you* relate to *yourself*.

TWO BRIEF COMMENTS

Clean it up! Meaning, if your integrity is out, get it back in. If you told someone you were going to do something, do it or revoke your promise. Being transparent lightens your load.

Be generous to yourself (and others). No one gave you (or them) a playbook and said, "Here is how to win at the game of life." Now that you have a sense of what is needed, what is possible, you have the opportunity to play full out.

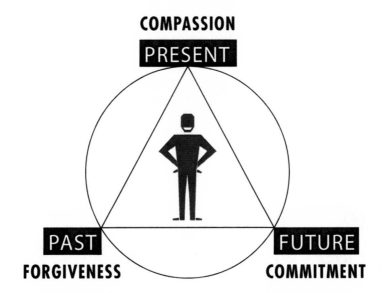

TRANSITIONS PROCESS: A Powerful/Generous Place to Stand Is in the Intersection of Forgiveness, Compassion, and Commitment

15

THE TRANSITIONS PROCESS IN ORGANIZATIONS

Warren Bennis, the author of several classic leadership books, including *Becoming a Leader* and *An Invented Life,* had it right when he said, "Leadership is ultimately about the relationship between the leader as individual and the organization." Self-exploration and reflection must be part of any successful leader's journey and makeup.

I have been fortunate to work with hundreds of leaders in business, government, the arts, the military, and even space exploration. Almost without exception, they were able to utilize the Transitions Process and have a positive effect on the health and success of their enterprise.

Getting people aligned on a vision or common purpose is one of the primary roles of a leader. However, knowing this and accomplishing it are two different things. The task of fulfilling the vision or purpose falls on the shoulders of management, who are responsible for making it happen.

When they are successful, when targets are met, everyone benefits and Wall Street smiles. But what about the times when things are not working? What happens then? Often, organizational difficulties are the result of external factors. For Halliburton, the price of oil drops dramatically. For Texas Instruments, a competitor develops a new chip that's cheaper or faster than any product they have. Other times, the problems stem from within—lackluster marketing and sales, poor communication resulting in delays in production, poor quality control, and so forth.

Whatever the source, it is not unusual at these times for morale to falter, accompanied by lots of nonproductive behavior (pointing fingers, blame, excuses, justification, concern for one's job, etc.). So management attacks the problem by reaching into their standard tool kit and taking various actions to turn things around. They redeclare their vision and goals. They revise the strategy and the budget. They restructure parts of the organization and improve processes. They conduct team building, communication, and management training.

But then what? What if everything being done still doesn't produce the needed breakthrough? The answer may surprise you. What I have noticed in addressing hundreds of these situations is that the breakthrough occurs when someone steps up and takes a stand for producing the desired outcome.

Dennis was the senior VP of a major financial institution. They were being clobbered by the competition's credit card division. He claimed the way to compete and win was not the old way of competing on price but the exact opposite. He said, "Let's create an elite card that you have to pay four times as much as any existing card out there. And let's make sure we offer great, unique benefits to the cardholder." Twenty years later, the Platinum Card is still the standard in the industry.

Repeatedly, we see that someone leads the path to success and usually does so by taking a stand: "This will work. I will get it done." And then they and others take the actions that make it happen. Perhaps the most important aspect of the Transitions Process in an organizational setting is the optimization of the relationship between individual responsibility and ongoing corporate performance.

Dwight is CEO of PPR, a health-care recruiting firm constantly recognized as one of the best in the industry. He said, "It's my job to unlock the potential of my employees. I have to create an environment where they can do their best. We value our employees' commitments and contributions and recognize the strength of our team is the key to our competitive advantage."

Unlocking an individual's potential often requires making an investment in that person's development. Many of my corporate engagements have centered on the development of key employees.

Stephen was an up-and-coming young executive. He graduated from MIT and was heir apparent for the CEO role in a multibillion-dollar manufacturing company. The current CEO requested that I help develop Stephen to be ready to succeed him as CEO in two years, when he intended to retire. During the next four months, Stephen went through the Transitions Process, and his transformation was obvious to everyone.

Instead of telling people what and how, he began asking for suggestions and input. Instead of only conducting one-on-one meetings with his direct reports, he saw the value of team meetings where everyone could benefit from what others were working on and accomplishing.

This is not taking anything away from Stephen's success prior to doing the Transitions Process. He was extremely successful in making his financial targets and getting things done. But the current CEO knew that to be successful at the next level, Stephen needed to transform his relationship with others, communicate more effectively, delegate more efficiently, and trust others to run with their accountabilities.

One year later, the CEO again approached me and requested that I put Stephen through an advanced level of the Transitions Process. He was now approaching his final year as CEO and felt that in six months he would have to introduce his successor to the thousands of employees in the company. He wasn't sure everyone would accept Stephen, especially since several others were coveting the role.

So Stephen and I started anew. We identified several goals:
- To be recognized as a leader by peers
- To lead meetings more effectively
- To empower and develop talent
- To generate confidence in his leadership style and abilities

How did we accomplish all this? Not by trying to change or fix Stephen. He had all the tools needed from previously completing the Transitions Process. The key was to create projects for each of the goals and objectives and empower others to fulfill the tasks. The current CEO knew Stephen was ready when Stephen came to him and requested to take on several of the CEO's key accountabilities.

Stephen went from following orders and doing the bidding of the current CEO to creating himself and presenting himself as the one who would be accountable for those key metrics. Having made the requests, having taken on those metrics and creating his own relationship with essential key executives and the board, he demonstrated he was ready to meet the challenge.

> You don't have to be an executive to take a stand and make a difference.

Rami, who recently completed the Transitions Process, was a finance officer for a training and development company in Los Angeles. On several occasions, Rami's month-end records and the corresponding bank statements did not match up. Although it wasn't a great amount of money, it was troublesome, because the president of the company was losing confidence in all the financials. He could never get resolution on why there were discrepancies.

Rami went to the bank and got a commitment from the

account manager that the discrepancies would be cleared up in forty-eight hours. When Rami returned to the bank that Wednesday, the account manager apologized and said he didn't have time to get to it. He reassured Rami it would be complete by Friday. Guess what? On Friday, it was the same story, along with a new promise to have things cleared up by the next week.

Reluctantly, Rami started out of the bank but got as far as the revolving door. The "old Rami" would have been reasonable and accepted the excuse. This time, though, she took a stand and was unwilling to go back to her office and face the president of her company empty-handed. She reentered the bank, went to the bank manager's office, explained what had happened, and said it was unacceptable and that perhaps she needed to find another banking institution to do business with. The bank manager gave Rami his word he would have the issues handled by the following Tuesday.

When Rami returned to the bank on Tuesday, the bank manager saw her walk in and invited her into his office. He said, "Thank you for bringing this my attention. When I dug a little deeper, I found out that the entire customer service department was in chaos. I had all the customer service reps and account managers in all weekend, and we completely restructured our process. I have all your questions and discrepancies resolved and hope this helps. We are sorry for any inconvenience we caused you."

One person taking a stand not only made a difference in her company but also impacted the performance of a major banking institution.

THE POWER OF TEAM

The toughest part of forming a team is in the beginning. Going from a group of individuals doing what they want, to an aligned team acting collaboratively on behalf of a shared commitment, is harder than it looks.

Being on a team requires being up to something that is worth being up to. It also requires that people be willing to move beyond their comfort zones and to surrender their personal beliefs and points of view for the good of the whole.

This is where the Transitions Process can make a huge difference. Team members have a new and powerful way of interacting with each other when they listen and speak intentionally for the future and when conversations have a shared commitment, partnership, belonging, contribution, inclusiveness, and possibility.

When these distinctions are learned in a group setting, it is often a deeper and more profound learning than when they are learned on an individual basis. Perhaps that is a function of the opportunity participants have to observe each other and to support each other when some part of the conversation is difficult to understand.

Each person comes to the group with a unique set of internal conversations. Since people's actions are a function of their internal conversations, and the results people produce are a function of the actions they take, people are encouraged to not withhold their concerns, problems, or, for that matter, great new ideas. All of the above are part of the solution. When someone is stuck, it's far more productive for that person to let others know they are stuck. That isn't a sign of weakness. It's an invitation to others to contribute.

Lenny worked with one of the major oil companies as a senior engineer maintaining a refinery. His team was falling behind in scheduled maintenance and repairs. To make matters worse, it was northern Canada, and winter was approaching. Temperatures would eventually drop to negative fifty degrees Fahrenheit. Lenny's manager was pressing him for answers and results, but he couldn't find any way to catch up.

Lenny and his team of fifteen mechanics went through the Transitions Program in July. At first, the mood of the group was one of anger and frustration. People were working as hard as they could. What more could be expected of them? When asked to list the reasons they were falling behind, they filled up several sheets on the flipchart. Some of the reasons they listed were as follows:

- They didn't have the right parts.
- Management didn't listen to them when they said a piece of equipment was in need of repair and needed to come off the line.
- Repair orders were getting lost and misplaced.
- Requests for equipment manufacturers to come and provide support were ignored.
- Their team had been downsized twice in the past year.

Clearly, bemoaning the past was not going to bring about the desired results. After a couple of days of training, they were asked, "If this is going to work out, if we are going to catch up with the scheduled maintenance and repairs, what would have to happen?"

They were encouraged to simply suggest possible solutions without having to figure out how to actually implement the solutions. Suggestions included the following:

- Create a list of all the needed work and prioritize based on risk of interruption of production.
- Get management to provide additional administrative support for ordering parts and maintaining files.
- Have daily meetings first thing in the morning to share information and request support from each other.
- Have meetings at shift changes to let the next team know what needs to get done.

- Create a game with goals and specific outcomes to be achieved.
- Shift work schedules around to match the times when the equipment is least used.
- Prioritize outdoor repairs and maintenance to be done before winter sets in.
- Request some of the furloughed workers be returned to the job, even if only temporarily.
- Give management a list of equipment that should be discarded rather than repaired.
- Delegate a project leader to make the requests to management and keep everyone informed.

Just identifying these possibilities raised their morale dramatically. After all, some of the suggestions could be acted on immediately, including delegating a project leader, creating a game with goals, and having daily and shift-change meetings, to name a few. The best news was that, through the training process, they actually became a team.

The workers' shift in attitude inspired management. They were more than willing to listen to the suggestions and even respond with support, including rehiring a small number of additional workers.

By the time winter came (that would have been in October), the gap was dramatically closed. What they couldn't get done because of the weather would have to wait until spring. But they now had a totally different relationship with the work, management, and each other.

16
YES, WE CAN

Living in the twenty-first century has been much like riding a roller coaster. It feels like you need to cling tightly to the safety bar to avoid being thrown from your seat. Wall Street, terrorism, and extreme weather events are just a few of the disruptions that can overwhelm our sense of safety and security.

But a renewed creative energy is also being unleashed, even if it is in its early stages. I firmly believe the future we desire is available, if we have the tools and are committed to grabbing it. The Transitions Process is predicated on the observation that the natural tendency for all human beings is to build, create, and open up new territory for our self-expression. When we are governed not by fear, anxiety, overconfidence, or underconfidence but simply by a future we are committed to, great things can occur.

My clients range from being extraordinarily successful to sorting their way through career and personal challenges. By any measure, almost without exception, their lives have changed for the better after going through this process. I like to say that at the completion of the process, you find yourself at the intersection of authentic joy and success.

The Transitions Process is essentially the restart button that most people yearn for; they want to be both successful and confident they are contributing to the people and things that matter most. This program is not a formula. It is a catalyst for them to find that they can listen to and hear a very different internal conversation. That new way of listening can give them access to their dreams.

Our lives are a gift that we may use in any way we choose. It's up to us to make those choices deliberately. This recognition comes to people in unequal degrees and levels of clarity. At one end of the spectrum, it's a momentary insight, an aha moment, a sense of being at one with the universe. But given the right guidance and fostering, it can also become a more permanent state, integrating into all aspects of our lives.

We become filled with the knowledge that our lives ultimately belong to a much higher purpose, a bigger game. At first, there is just an appreciation that the game actually exists. But later, we learn to play and influence the flow of the game itself. Once experienced, the feeling is never forgotten, and it can serve as a touchstone and guide in uncertain times ahead.

Going forward armed with a sense of authentic freedom and a vision of some desired future, the human spirit is a wonderful, magical, powerful energy to behold.

How wonderful? Here is what playwright George Bernard Shaw once said:

This is the true joy in life, the being used for a purpose recognized by yourself as a mighty one. Being a force of nature instead of a feverish, selfish clot of ailments and grievances, complaining that the world will not devote itself to making you happy. I am of the opinion that my life belongs to the community, and as long as I live, it is my privilege to do for it what I can. I want to be more thoroughly used up when I die, for the harder I work, the more I live. I rejoice in life for its own sake. Life is no brief candle to me. It is the sort of splendid torch which I have got hold of for the moment, and I want to make it burn as brightly as possible before handing it on to future generations.

Inventor and author Buckminster Fuller once wrote, "To change something, build a new model that makes the existing model obsolete."

That's really what I have been writing about in this entire book—not just change, but transformation of self, those around us, and ultimately, if we are successful, society as a whole. Once you empower your own freedom to choose what your future will be, you are essentially done with yourself. Yes, you will have to continue working on *being* and becoming a match for your core values and commitments. Living your life is a journey, not a destination.

But the real opportunity now is to transform the world around you. Whether it's through technology, as demonstrated by Steve Jobs of Apple and Elon Musk of Tesla, or through committed involvement, as demonstrated by Lynne and Bill Twist taking a stand for saving the rain forest, there is no constraint to what's possible.

Begin a new business. Repair existing relationships. Launch new ones. Start an NGO. Make a radical career shift that recognizes fresh core values and revitalizes old ones. There is no end to the possibilities and no limit to where you can go, because the joy is now in the journey itself. The destination is almost incidental.

Here's another Buckminster Fuller quote: "How would you live if you thought humanity depended on it?"

And here is the final answer I have for you . . . *it does!*

RESOURCES

For further information on *If I Can, You Can* and the related areas below, visit:

www.ifican-ucan.com or

www.transitionsinstitute.com:

- Appearances and speaking engagements

- One- or two-day seminars on the 'principles of living successfully'

- One-on-one coaching consultations

- Personal and Professional Transitions programs

- Corporate Transitions program information

To email the author: dzelman@transitionsinstitute.com

To enlist the services of Dr. David Zelman, go to:

www.transitionsinstitute.com or call 214-528-9401.

CPSIA information can be obtained at www.ICGtesting.com
Printed in the USA
LVOW11s2226260216

476829LV00001B/1/P